THE MYSTERY IN THE
DROOD FAMILY

THE MYSTERY IN THE DROOD FAMILY

BY

MONTAGU SAUNDERS

Cambridge :
at the University Press
1914

CAMBRIDGE
UNIVERSITY PRESS

University Printing House, Cambridge CB2 8BS, United Kingdom

Cambridge University Press is part of the University of Cambridge.

It furthers the University's mission by disseminating knowledge in the pursuit of
education, learning and research at the highest international levels of excellence.

www.cambridge.org
Information on this title: www.cambridge.org/9781107586048

First published 1914
First paperback edition 2015

A catalogue record for this publication is available from the British Library

ISBN 978-1-107-58604-8 Paperback

TO

A. K. S.

PREFACE

IT needs a considerable amount of assurance to add yet another book to the comparatively long list of those which have been written upon the subject of Dickens's unfinished story, and it is no sufficient justification to assert that the writer is sincerely convinced that his contribution to the discussion will afford some assistance in the solution of the problem, seeing that practically everyone who has ventilated his ideas upon the subject has expressed a similar conviction. Proctor, for instance, who was the first to examine *Edwin Drood* in a quasi-scientific way, was absolutely satisfied that in identifying Datchery with Edwin, he had discovered the "mystery" which Dickens had taken such pains to hide, and so strongly did he feel that his solution was correct, that he exhibited considerable impatience with those who failed to swallow it whole. Mr J. Cuming Walters, again, the originator of the highly ingenious

Helena-Datchery theory, is equally convinced
that he has unearthed Dickens's secret, and,
like Proctor, he has supported his views by
means of numerous arguments drawn from the
text, which, if they do not carry conviction
to every mind, are nevertheless sufficiently
weighty to call for very careful examination,
more particularly as they have succeeded in
securing as adherents of the theory two such
acute critics and eminent scholars as Dr Henry
Jackson and Sir W. R. Nicoll. In these
circumstances the present writer considers
that it would be presumption on his part to
express any definite opinion as to the accuracy
of his own conclusions, and he feels that some
apology is needed for the dogmatism which,
upon a re-reading of this little essay, seems
to him at times to be only too apparent.
His excuse must be, that when an idea takes
possession of the mind so completely as to
become almost an obsession, it is liable to
warp the judgment to such an extent that
even the possibility of any other view being
reasonably entertained seems too remote to
require serious consideration, and as this book
was written red-hot under the influence of

such an idea, it is inevitable that it must be tainted with the fault of over-assurance. The same cause has also led him to criticise the work of other enquirers more freely than he otherwise would have done, and certainly more confidently than his literary inexperience warrants, and accordingly he hastens to assure those who may think it worth while to examine and dissect his own arguments, that he will not resent any strictures, however severe, that they may feel called upon to pass on the views which he has enunciated or developed. It is hardly necessary for him to state that he is painfully aware of his literary short-comings, and that he asserts no pretensions to style, being satisfied if he has succeeded in expressing his views clearly, and in bringing out the full force of the arguments which he believes can be adduced in their support ; he trusts, therefore, that such criticisms as may be expressed with reference to his work, will be addressed rather to the matter than the form of it, and he will sincerely welcome criticism of this nature, as tending to test and evaluate the strength of his arguments and the validity of his various theories. However confidently he may appear to have expressed the views which he has advanced, he hopes that he has a sufficiently open mind fully to appreciate the force of the objections which may be urged against them, and he is not so strongly wedded to any particular theory as to be desirous of supporting it against the weight of evidence. His sole desire is to discover, or to assist in discovering, the true solution of Dickens's puzzle, and if his own ideas are shown to be untenable, he will have no hesitation in abandoning them.

If, however, it should be considered that he has been fortunate enough to have hit upon the true solution of any of the numerous problems which *Edwin Drood* presents, he would point out that he has enjoyed the immense advantage of being in a position to profit by the work of prior investigators, by whom the ground has been so thoroughly surveyed and minutely examined as in several cases almost to compel him, by the mere process of exhaustion, to adopt the conclusions at which he has arrived. As one instance of this may be cited the identification of Datchery, and as another, his interpretation of the enigmatic picture forming the lower part of the original wrapper of the monthly Parts, which has given rise to almost as many readings as there have been commentators. The suggestion now advanced with regard to this picture is not, and, in the circumstances, could not be, original, but in the opinion of the writer it gains greater probability both from the fact that it is the logical outcome of the main plot which he has outlined, and from the circumstance that it explains and justifies the much-debated title of Chapter XIV. In the same way, many of the arguments which he has employed to support his own theories, or to combat those of earlier enquirers, have no doubt been presented before, and probably with far superior clarity and greater cogency, and he accordingly hesitates to advance a claim to originality in respect of any one of them, but as his first-hand acquaintance with the literature upon the subject does not extend beyond the magazine articles of Proctor, and the works of Sir W. R. Nicoll and Dr Henry Jackson, he may perhaps be acquitted of having consciously plagiarised the ideas of other writers. He desires, however, to acknowledge his very great indebtedness to Sir W. R. Nicoll, without the aid of whose scholarly and exhaustive book this little essay could hardly have been written, and although the conclusions at which he has arrived are in most instances totally at variance with those adopted by Sir William, yet his obligations to that work are in no wise diminished on that account.

It is only due to the " Dickens Fellowship " to state that this essay owes its origin to the fact that the writer's attention was drawn to the fascinating problem of the discovery of Dickens's secret by the press notices of the mock trial of John Jasper for the murder of Edwin Drood, which that society organised in January last. While obviously it would not be fair to try and shift on to other shoulders the responsibility which naturally devolves upon a writer who is venturesome enough to advance a new theory concerning Dickens's plot, it is impossible to dispute the fact that the society must be held accountable for the interest in the problem which the trial aroused, and to that extent, therefore, it must be prepared to accept responsibility for the natural consequences of its act.

Lastly, the author wishes to express his gratitude to the Syndics of the Cambridge University Press for having kindly undertaken the publication of this book.

M. S.

Sept. 1914.

CONTENTS

CHAPTER I

DICKENS'S NEW IDEA

DICKENS'S unfinished story presents us not with one, but with many mysteries, none of which, I believe, has yet been satisfactorily solved. Efforts have, up to the present, been principally directed to the solution of the problems connected with the identity of Datchery, the death or escape of Edwin, and the identity of the opium woman, and the main idea of the book has been either completely overlooked, or treated as of secondary importance only; logically, I think the process should have been reversed, and that the theme around which Dickens wove his romance should have received primary attention, inasmuch as discovery of the leading motive might possibly throw light upon the minor mysteries, and accordingly I shall endeavour in the first place to ascertain whether there is any material from which the nature of the main theme can fairly be inferred, regarding this, in fact, as the main mystery.

So far as regards external evidence, we find Dickens writing to Forster : " I have a very curious and new idea for my new story ; not a communicable idea (or the interest of the book would be gone) but a very strong one, though difficult to work." I lay some stress upon the word " new," first, because Mr R. A. Proctor, who identifies Datchery with Edwin, considers the main theme of the story to be the tracking of Jasper, the supposed murderer, by Edwin, his supposed victim, an idea which Dickens had admittedly already used on several previous occasions, and secondly, because, as Sir W. Robertson Nicoll points out, the idea of a young girl assuming a disguise had been used in *No Name*. I think, therefore, that if Dickens had meant either of those ideas to form his main plot, he would hardly have qualified it as new, and for that reason I suggest that neither Proctor's nor Mr Cuming Walters's theory, even if correct, which I doubt, would satisfactorily explain Dickens's statement quoted above. The supporters of the Helena-Datchery view certainly partly avoid this particular objection, as the assumption by a young girl of the character of such a man as Datchery was, I think, new, so far as Dickens was concerned; but I hardly think that Dickens would have said of an idea of this nature that it was "very curious" or that it was "not a communicable idea" or "a very strong one, though difficult to work." In the first place, I cannot see that the "interest of the book would be gone," even although we knew Helena to be Datchery; in the second place, a craftsman like Dickens would hardly have considered such an idea as "difficult to work," and lastly, I am convinced that he would not have qualified it as "very strong." The difficult-to-work objection seems the gravest, as there would seem to have been no great difficulty either in effectually disguising Helena, had Dickens set out with the intention of doing so, or in locating her in Cloisterham, instead of taking her up to London, as he does, but both the "very curious" and "very strong" expressions appear to me also to be quite inapplicable to the Helena-Datchery hypothesis.

Neither of the theories of attempted-murder-and-escape, and murder-and-discovery-by-the-ring, seems to me in itself to merit Dickens's description of "very curious and new, incommunicable, very strong, difficult to work," and I am consequently of opinion that we must look elsewhere for "the plan," as Sir W. R. Nicoll puts it, which "Dickens had in his mind, and half revealed and half concealed." The first likely suggestion that we find in the story itself is in Chapter III, where animal magnetism and two states of consciousness are referred to, and this suggestion is somewhat strengthened by the scene at the piano described in Chapter VII, by Crisparkle's memorable night-walk, which we find in Chapter XVI, and finally by the whole of the conversation between Jasper and Rosa, set out in detail in Chapter XIX. It is not at all improbable that animal magnetism was in some way intended to be used by Dickens; it would certainly be "incommunicable, or the interest of the book would be gone," but I cannot say whether the idea would have been new at the time *Edwin Drood* was being written, nor whether at that time it would have been thought "very curious." At the same time it hardly appears to me to merit the epithet " a very strong one " employed by Dickens himself, and personally, I should be inclined to regard it as easy, rather than difficult, to work ; that, however, is purely a matter of opinion, and I cannot pretend to the slightest authority on this point. On the whole, however, while admitting that animal magnetism may quite possibly have something to do with the plot, and while, like Mr Grewgious, keeping an eye on every direction that may present itself, I incline to the opinion that the suggestion that I am now about to put forward embodies Dickens's leading idea.

In the notes which Dickens made for the chapters which he wrote, we find, under Chapter XII, the following entry : " Jasper's diary ? Yes," and again under Chapter XVI, a similar note : " Jasper's diary." The notes for Chapter XII are, comparatively speaking, long, and deal with so many points that, in my opinion, it would not have been possible to dispose of them all in one chapter ; we find, as a fact, that in Chapter X, although there is nothing in the notes to this effect, Jasper produces his diary to Crisparkle, wherein he has set out his fears for Edwin at the hands of Neville, and this, I take it, disposes of the note under Chapter xII. The production of the diary to Crisparkle at this point, is, in my view, evidently intended to prepare the reader for the later production at the end of Chapter xVI, so that it may then appear natural, and not excite any particular attention; if this supposition be correct, Dickens certainly succeeded in achieving his object. Under the notes for Chapter xVI, immediately after the words " Jasper's diary," we find, " I devote myself to his destruction," and if we turn to the end of that chapter, where the quotation from the diary appears in full, we see how this last phrase has been expanded: " I now swear, and record the oath on this page, that I never more will discuss this mystery with any human creature until I hold the clue to it in my hand. That I will never relax in my secrecy or in my search. That I will fasten the crime of the murder of my dear dead boy upon the murderer. That I will devote myself to his destruction."

Now, if Jasper were a murderer (or intended to be a murderer) and desired to put

Crisparkle off the scent, the earlier production
of his diary to the latter, before Edwin's
disappearance, would have sufficed to attain
this object; from this point of view, the
communication at the end of Chapter XVI,
made, as Dickens states, " without one spoken
word," really took the matter no further.
This consideration, in conjunction with
Dickens's notes, leads me to the belief that the
entry in Jasper's diary last referred to, was
quoted in order to convey something to the
reader, if he could only perceive it. Can we
discover what that something was ? Suppose,
now, that Dickens meant every line and every
word of this entry to be read literally, as
conveying the simple truth; that he meant
it to be fulfilled word for word, and letter
for letter; and suppose also that Jasper was,
or thought himself to be (for it does not very
much matter for this purpose which view we
adopt) the murderer. We are forced, upon
these lines, to " a very curious and very strong
idea, difficult to work, and not communicable
without endangering the interest of the story";
namely, the idea of a murderer attempting
and intending to fasten his crime on to

another, but in reality *tracking himself*, and involuntarily putting the noose round his own neck ! So far as I am aware, such an idea was entirely new, and in Dickens's hands it would have been highly dramatic ; he would have seen and rejoiced in its possibilities, although we can quite understand that he would also have foreseen the difficulties of its treatment.

That Jasper was and had good reason for being at work endeavouring to fix the crime upon Neville, is plainly to be gathered from subsequent passages. First, there is the interview with Honeythunder, where the latter tells Crisparkle that he would be better employed in devoting himself to the discovery and punishment of the murderer than in leaving that duty to be undertaken by a layman, showing clearly that Jasper had been in communication with Honeythunder on this subject. (Dickens deleted this passage, for some unknown reason ; possibly desiring, as Honeythunder was a character he intended to utilise further, not to disclose the presumably close relations between him and Jasper. I think, by the way, that Honeythunder was present

at Mrs Crisparkle's dinner-party, in order
that Jasper might make his acquaintance
naturally.) Next, there is the conversation
between Sapsea and Datchery (which Dickens
also deleted) in which Sapsea, Jasper's tool,
stated that there were more than suspicions,
all but certainties, of some one. Thirdly, there
is Jasper's own declaration to Rosa: "Mr Crisparkle knows under my hand that I have
devoted myself to the murderer's discovery
and destruction, *be he whom he might,* and that
I determined to discuss the mystery with no
one until I should hold the clue in which to
entangle the murderer as in a net. I have
since worked patiently to wind and wind it
round him ; *and it is slowly winding as I
speak.*" And lastly, there is the fact of
Jasper watching Neville, as Grewgious had
discovered. Jasper the murderer, whether in
deed or intention, Honeythunder the bully,
Sapsea the jackass, possibly also Bazzard the
fool, are all labouring to convict Neville of
the crime, a task in which we have every
reason for believing that they did not succeed ;
would it not be an excellent *dénouement* if
Jasper and his allies in this nefarious plot

merely succeeded in achieving the result
which Justice demands, namely, that of convicting Jasper himself of the deed ?

While there is not, and cannot be, any
direct evidence that this was the plot which
Dickens had in his mind, nevertheless I think
that I am justified in saying that it fits in
better with all the known facts than any of the
other theories yet advanced. In particular,
it satisfactorily explains Dickens's note to
Forster, in every detail, while it also supplies
a valid reason for the second production to
Crisparkle of Jasper's diary, a communication
which otherwise seems to me to be quite object-
less. I think it likely that Rosa's mother's
ring would have been used by Dickens as the
means for bringing about the desired end,—
as I shall show later on ; Jasper was to get
to hear of it, designedly or by accident, and,
meaning to place it in Neville's possession
secretly, was to attempt to gain possession of
it ; in the act of doing so he would be surprised (at Mrs Sapsea's tomb, possibly) by
the person knowing him to have the information, whereby Jasper's guilty knowledge would
be disclosed by his own act. We have to give

due weight to the emphatic words in Chapter
XIII, " a chain...gifted with invincible force
to hold and drag," and although of course
these words fit in, more or less well, with any
theory involving Jasper's discovery of the
existence and search for the ring, I hope to
be able to give them their true value.   I only
wish to point out here that there is no other
theory, so far as I am aware, than the one
I am advancing, which *necessitates* the removal of the ring by Jasper from its hiding-
place for any specific purpose.   He might, of
course, desire to abstract it so as to prevent
identification of the remains, if and when
discovered, but it appears to me that his
interest is really all the other way ; if he
desires to convict Neville otherwise than by
tracing the ring to his possession, it would
surely answer his purpose to allow the ring
to remain on the body, so that the identification may be certain when the corpse is discovered.   Proctor suggested that Jasper was
driven to remove the ring from the tomb,
because it was a fatal witness to his crime,
and that Grewgious and Edwin meant to
punish him by forcing him to go through the

terrible ordeal of groping in the dust of his
victim to recover the ring. Against this I
think I may fairly urge that Jasper would
have been satisfied that the chances of the
corpse being discovered or disturbed were so
small, that he would have taken the risk of
the simultaneous discovery of the ring, rather
than face such an ordeal; at the same time,
we must also not forget, as has indeed been
frequently pointed out, that Edwin must have
had about him other metal articles, such as
keys, buttons, and so on, which would have
led to the identification of the corpse just as
surely as the ring, so that on this ground also
Proctor's theory is weak. I think, therefore,
that my suggestion that Jasper was to attempt
to recover the ring in order to place it in
Neville's possession, is the more likely one,
and as it entirely fits in with my explanation
of Dickens's plot as a whole, it may be accepted
as a working hypothesis, in which case it
strongly corroborates my main position.

The page headings, if they are authentic,
also confirm my view; they are respectively,
" Mr Jasper's Diary," and " Mr Jasper regis-
ters a vow." In the former, stress is laid

upon the diary, in the latter upon Jasper's oath, and I think that it is a fair inference to draw, that it is to the oath itself that Dickens wished eventually to be able to point as embodying the " mystery " of his plot. The heading of Chapter XVI, " Devoted," also leads in the same direction, more particularly when it is remembered that a secondary meaning of the word, which we must assume was known to Dickens, is " given up to doom." Again, we find, according to Sir W. R. Nicoll, that upon the back of the number-plan for part four, Dickens had made this entry :

Edwin Disappears.

THE MYSTERY. DONE ALREADY.

This could not, of course, refer to the Datchery mystery, as that character does not appear until the next number, neither could it refer to the opium woman, about whom there is nothing really mysterious before Chapter XXIII. It might possibly relate to the manner of the murder, but I regard this as highly improbable on account of the first note quoted above, " Edwin Disappears." There is apparently, therefore, nothing left to which the words can reasonably be held to have been intended to apply, with the exception of the " mystery " contained in the last extract from Jasper's diary, and accordingly I regard this note as exceedingly strong corroborative evidence in support of my thesis.

But even this is not all. Sir W. R. Nicoll has set out, at page 57 of his most valuable book, *The Problem of Edwin Drood*—to which, once for all, I desire to acknowledge my extreme indebtedness for numerous details—the various titles for his new story which Dickens noted down but subsequently discarded. They may, perhaps, not unfairly be regarded as indicating the working of his mind at the different periods when they were jotted down, for I do not suppose that they were noted otherwise than at intervals. I transcribe the whole page here, with due acknowledgments.

Friday, Twentieth August 1869

	Gilbert Alfred Edwin
	Jasper Edwyn
	Michael Oswald
The loss of James Wakefield	Arthur
Edwyn	Selwyn
	Edgar
	Mr Honeythunder
	Mr Honeyblast
James's Disappearance	The Dean
	Mrs Dean
	Miss Dean

FLIGHT AND PURSUIT
  SWORN TO AVENGE IT
   ONE OBJECT IN LIFE
A KINSMAN'S DEVOTION
       THE TWO KINSMEN
The Loss of Edwyn Brood
  The Loss of Edwyn Brude
  The Mystery in the Drood Family
The Loss of Edwyn Drood
  The Flight of Edwyn Drood. Edwin Drood in Hiding
  The Loss of Edwin Drude.
The Disappearance of Edwin Drood
  The Mystery of Edwin Drood.
    Dead? Or Alive?

I take it that we here see Dickens vacil-
lating between two opposing ideas, uncertain
whether his title shall relate to his main

mystery, or shall be so framed as to draw
attention to the secondary one, with the
object, no doubt, of putting the reader off
the scent ; the titles vary according as the
one view or the other for the moment obtains
predominance. The first title contains no
reference to Dickens's main theme, neither
does the second. (I assume that the word
" Edwin " was never meant to be a title at
all.) In the third (the first printed in capi-
tals), we get an indirect allusion to the
principal mystery, which is more marked in
the fourth and fifth, and less definitely
prominent in the sixth, while in the seventh
it has almost vanished. In the eighth, attention is diverted entirely from the main mystery,
and Dickens reverts to his original intention,
and seeks to bring the disappearance of Drood
into prominence, and the same remark applies
to the following title. The tenth is again
on somewhat different lines, inasmuch as it
leaves the nature of the mystery a much more
open question. The eleventh is identical with
the eighth, except for a slight change of name,
and calls for no comment. In the twelfth
and thirteenth we meet with yet another idea,

namely, a definite suggestion that Edwin might not have been killed after all, but I take it that Dickens considered that he was not justified in actually misleading his readers in this way, and he therefore reverted in the fourteenth and fifteenth to the original indefiniteness of the first and second. The next is the title actually adopted, and the last, while obviously inappropriate as a title, nevertheless shows that Dickens had finally adopted the view that the main mystery was not the one to which attention must be drawn. It is intensely interesting to observe how in these titles the one theme disappears as the other comes into prominence, and I cannot conceive of any other explanation than that Dickens gradually came to the decision to keep his " new idea " as much as possible in the background, and so came to lay more and more stress in his title upon what, after all, he intended to be merely a secondary mystery.

I am of course aware that, according to Forster, the originality of the story was " to consist in the review of the murderer's career by himself at the close, when its temptations were to be dwelt upon as if not he, the culprit,

but some other man, were the tempted."
While admitting the weight of Forster's testimony, and not denying that Dickens probably
did intend to review Jasper's career in this
way, I cannot convince myself that this was
really his *central* idea, the one which he
qualified as " very curious, not communicable,
but very strong, and difficult to work." I
cannot help thinking that he must have had
in his mind when writing to Forster, not
a mere episode, which is in effect what such
a review would have been, but a theme or
plot which was to colour and direct the whole
story, and I confess to feeling considerable
surprise that hitherto this view has apparently
not obtruded itself upon some one of the
numerous and able critics who have so
minutely examined the book. While not
desiring to appear dogmatic, I feel very
strongly that the view I have advanced is so
inherently probable and so entirely appropriate to Dickens's statement to Forster, as
well as to his general manner, that even if
there were no intrinsic evidence in support of
it, I should hold that I had made out my case.
But when we find, as I have endeavoured to

show, that my contention is also borne out by independent intrinsic testimony, we arrive, I venture to assert, at almost mathematical certainty. Absolute proof, of course, we can never expect to get, but if a " backward light " such as Dickens referred to, has been disclosed, I consider that I have every reason for maintaining that I have succeeded in showing, in his own words, " what everything has been working to," or, to use the expression of Sir W. R. Nicoll, in discovering the plan which Dickens had " in his mind, that he half revealed and half concealed."

That my solution is correct, the sequel will, I think, show, inasmuch as several points which have hitherto remained doubtful appear to me, in the light of it, to allow of obvious explanation, but even if my ideas upon other questions do not meet with acceptance, I do not think that my main position will be invalidated.

Let us see how, in the light of my solution, Dickens's main plot works out. As early as Chapter II we find that Jasper has a hidden skeleton in his house ; what that skeleton is we do not learn, either then or later, but we do learn that he hates his vocation, that he is troubled with some stray sort of " ambition, aspiration, restlessness, dissatisfaction " which Edwin is asked to take as a warning, but refuses. At the end of Chapter III, when Edwin remarks, " I fancy I can distinguish Jack's voice," Rosa unaccountably urges " Take me back at once." At the end of Chapter v we read (whether appropriately or not) " John Jasper stands looking down upon him (Edwin) his unlighted pipe in his hand, for some time, with a fixed and deep attention." In Chapter VII we have the scene of Jasper at the piano, and Rosa overcome by his magnetic influence ; while in Chapter VIII Edwin and Neville, after being surprised by Jasper (who has furtively followed them from the nuns' house) in a state of incipient animosity, are brought by him into active quarrel, wherein Neville's conduct is characterised by Jasper to Crisparkle as " murderous."

So far, things are pretty plain ; Jasper's " ambition " is Rosa, and sub-consciously, she is aware of it. The " warning " to Edwin, which he neither understands nor heeds, is that he shall not stand in Jasper's path, and

the latter is therefore forced to meditate even
criminal means for removing his unconscious
rival. In Dickens's own words, there is a
quarrel, fomented by Jasper, and he *lays his
ground*, not only by creating animosity between the two boys, but by maligning Neville
to Crisparkle, with the intention, no doubt,
of being able to throw suspicion upon him,
if occasion arises. At the end of Chapter x
(at the beginning of which we learn that, by
some mysterious means, the quarrel has been
magnified and spread about), Jasper learns
from Grewgious, first, that Rosa has hinted
no wish to be released from Edwin, secondly,
that he and Grewgious are " not wanted,"
and thirdly, that Edwin is to return at
Christmas to complete the preparations for
the marriage in May. After exhibiting considerable emotion, he winds up by remarking
to Grewgious " God save them both," thus
indicating more or less plainly that one of
them at least is in danger. Then Crisparkle
plays into his hands. Awakening him from
an opium-induced sleep in which he is evidently
meditating murder, Crisparkle informs Jasper
that he wants to establish peace between the

two young men, whereupon a very perplexed and perplexing expression takes hold of Jasper's face ; in other words, he is working out in his own mind how he can turn the situation to advantage. Crisparkle unconsciously " smooths the way for Jasper's plan," and the latter, realising how the fates are playing into his hand, first promises to bring about the required reconciliation, and then further traduces Neville by the production to Crisparkle of his diary, carefully prepared to shield himself in case of necessity.

Edwin's letter, which Jasper produces to Crisparkle on the third day after this conversation, while to all appearance a simple and innocent epistle, nevertheless appears to me to be a carefully concocted document, as, though it is intended to convey the impression that Edwin fixes the appointment for Christmas Eve, it is plain on a careful reading that it is an acceptance of an invitation by Jasper for that day ; Jasper has laid his ground for the murder, and will use Neville as the scapegoat. To carry out his intention he makes the nocturnal expedition with Durdles, on which he determines upon the manner of the murder, and makes his preparations with methodical forethought.

In Chapter XIII we get the last interview between Rosa and Edwin on December 23rd, when Edwin, unmindful of Rosa's singular emotion on hearing him speak of Jasper, agrees not to mention anything to him of their decision to part, but to allow the news to be broken to him by Grewgious, who had promised Rosa to come to her at Christmas, if written to. Then we are told, with particular emphasis, that Edwin, in deciding not to give Rosa the betrothal ring which Grewgious had handed to him, forged a wonderful chain, gifted with invincible force to hold and drag. From the fact that Dickens not only makes no secret of the retention by Edwin of this ring, but ostentatiously directs the reader's attention to it, we may safely infer that the part the ring is to play is not the part which one would naturally be led to attribute to it. The same remark holds good with regard to the disclosure by the jeweller that Jasper was acquainted with all the articles of jewellery which Edwin wore.

After Edwin's scene with the opium-

woman, and Jasper's reassuring conversation
with Crisparkle, we finally arrive at the windy
night and the murder and alarm. Neville,
who had gone on a walking tour, is arrested
and brought back at the instigation of Jasper,
examined before Mr Sapsea, and taken charge
of by Crisparkle. Jasper searches the river
ostentatiously, and takes an early opportunity
of getting rid of Edwin's watch and scarf-pin
by dropping them in the weir. Then comes
his famous interview with Grewgious, when
he learns that he has committed a useless
murder, and swoons away. Close upon that
follows what Dickens calls his " artful use of
the communication on his recovery," namely,
his suggestion that, after all, Edwin may not
be dead, the object of which is no doubt to
prevent Grewgious drawing the obvious inference from his breakdown. But he very
soon has good cause to alter this attitude,
for, in addition to learning from Grewgious
that he has killed Edwin to no purpose, he
now learns from Crisparkle that the man he
should have killed is Neville. This news
turns him paler ; he has bungled his case,
killed the wrong man, and got rid of the only

articles which would have enabled him to fasten the crime upon his new rival. He is at a loss how to act. Note very carefully all that Dickens says in Chapter xvi, after the finding of the watch and pin ; every suggestion is so obvious, so frankly stated, that it is assuredly self-evident that he was putting forward merely what every one would have thought of at once. And yet it is all true, word for word, as is also the entry in Jasper's diary with which the chapter concludes, in which he " devotes " himself to the destruction of the murderer. What, then, is the " mystery " except this " devotion," and what is the object of the ring, except to serve as the instrument for bringing about the self-destruction of the murderer, in strict conformity with his oath, through the attempt to use it as evidence for the inculpation of his rival ? To me it all seems as clear as noon-day. Dickens's very frankness has thrown his commentators off the track, and they have followed every false scent which he cunningly threw out, while overlooking the clue which he took no pains to hide, and therefore hid most successfully. " These are the ways of Providence, of which ways all art is but a little imitation."

Although I propose to defer until later the full consideration of the grounds upon which that acute critic, Dr Henry Jackson, bases his acceptance of Mr J. Cuming Walters's theory that Datchery is Helena in disguise, I nevertheless think that this is a convenient place to comment very shortly upon such of his views as do not bear solely upon the question of the identity of Datchery. Dr Jackson recognises that Dickens intended to keep his readers in doubt about Drood's fate, and he even refers to some of the tentative titles as evidence in support of this view, but it does not seem to have occurred to him that Dickens's difficulty in his search for an appropriate title could have any definite connexion with his real plot, and he fails to notice the significance of many of the discarded titles. Forster's statement that not only the identity of the person murdered, but also the locality of the crime and the man who committed it were to be identified by means of the ring, is fully accepted by him, and he also duly notes Dickens's emphatic declaration respecting the

" chain " forged by Edwin's determination to
retain the ring, but he gets no nearer to the
real import of these hints than to suggest
(page 8, note) that an advertisement for the
ring might draw the murderer to the place
where the body was made away with. In
short, like Proctor, Mr Walters, and Sir W. R.
Nicoll, he fails to notice that the " mystery "
is " done already " at the end of Chapter xiv,
and he is accordingly constrained to look for
it where it is not, in accordance, no doubt,
with Dickens's intentions. Having no thread
to guide him through the labyrinth, Dr
Jackson, notwithstanding his extremely acute
critical faculty, and his extraordinary knowledge of the text, is consequently compelled
to adopt a theory concerning the " mystery "
against which there seemed to him to be conclusive evidence, until he discovered that by
effecting a transposition of Chapter xviii, he
could get rid of the difficulty. As I shall
endeavour to show later, this transposition is
not only unwarranted, but it does not even
achieve its object, as it leaves quite unex-
plained a subsequent reference to Helena
which makes it impossible that Dickens could

have intended us to believe that she was at
Cloisterham ; I only raise the point here,
however, for the purpose of showing that
Dr Jackson's views may be unconsciously
coloured by his chronological investigations,
which, in his opinion, derive support from
a doubt expressed by Dickens to his sister-
in-law respecting the Datchery assumption in
the fifth number.   This, then, being the state
of matters regarding Dr Jackson's views upon
the identity of Datchery, which he regards as
the " mystery," what arguments does he
adduce that can be accepted, in respect of the
nature of the real mystery ? Frankly speaking,
I find very little that is really helpful in this
direction. On page 10 he writes : " Crisparkle, impressed by Jasper's apparent can-
dour, tells his companions of Neville's second
outbreak of temper and of his jealousy...On
the strength of the discovery of the watch
and shirt-pin, Jasper declares himself convinced that Drood has been murdered, and
devotes himself to the destruction of the
murderer."   It is curious to notice how he
here misses the real point, namely, the discovery by Jasper that " Codlin's the *enemy*,

not Short," whereby he is induced to pursue
Neville relentlessly in order to remove him
also from his path. This pursuit of Neville
was of course strictly necessary for the due
carrying out of Dickens's plot, but it is difficult
to understand how the true significance of it
has failed to be realised, either by Dr Jackson
or any other writer. What is particularly
astonishing in a scholar of Dr Jackson's
eminence, is his omission to observe from
Dickens's repeated use of the word "devotion"
that he must have meant to attach to it some
special significance, which can be no other
than that derived from its original classical
meaning. Once noticed, this would straightway have given the necessary clue, but the
apparently obvious suggestion is never taken.

Dr Jackson, in discussing whether Drood
was effectually murdered or not, inclines to
the opinion that Jasper did achieve his purpose,
but that he changed his plans three times.
He first resolved to murder Drood himself,
and to hide the body in Mrs Sapsea's monument, but he was led to abandon this first
scheme by the discovery of Durdles's strange
" gift " and inconvenient habit of prowling

around his work. He next intended to stir up strife between Neville and Drood, so as to use the former for his cat's-paw for Edwin's destruction. Lastly, his third thought was to make away with Edwin in such a manner that Neville will be suspected of the crime. (By the way, how " warm " Dr Jackson sometimes gets without knowing it !) I venture to think that, from the time Jasper surprised Edwin and Neville on the brink of a quarrel, his mind was made up in favour of the third plan, and that he never entertained any other. With regard to the Sapsea monument, I cannot accept Dr Jackson's view, first, because Dickens very evidently did not introduce it into his story for ornamental purposes only, and secondly, because, equally evidently, it is necessary for the carrying out of the plot that Drood's body should be discovered, to which very end Durdles, with his curious " gift," is brought upon the scene. As regards the fact of the murder, I think it is clear, therefore, that Jasper succeeded, but I shall return to this point later.

With reference to the manner of the murder, while I have ventured to put forward a theory which is not in agreement with Dr Jackson's views, I readily admit that he is at least as likely to be right in his guess as I, and consequently I will not presume to criticise his hypothesis, beyond suggesting that he makes no use of Durdles's dinner-bundle, whereas, according to my theory, Jasper rifled it in order to obtain the necessary tools to execute the work which I think he did.

Half a year now elapses, Neville is established at Staple Inn, and Jasper, according to Dr Jackson, has also taken a room there, although I do not think that there is sufficient evidence to justify this statement. Jasper is evidently busy manufacturing evidence to incriminate Neville; in fact, for the due working out of the plot, he has to be, but Dr Jackson assumes that Grewgious, the man who searches out right and does right, who finds Neville chambers in Staple Inn, who detaches Bazzard for special duty, and who himself keeps a watch at Staple Inn upon Jasper's comings and goings, has nevertheless been sufficiently supine to take no active steps at Cloisterham to unmask Jasper. He

qualifies him as " a brigand and a wild beast
in combination" on July 4th, and yet we are
asked to believe that prior to that day he has
wilfully allowed the wild beast to be at large
without supervision or control of any sort, notwithstanding Grewgious's implacable dislike
of him dating from the preceding Christmas.
" No *two* of them " (*i.e.* the Staple Inn allies)
says Dr Jackson, " have set a watch upon
Jasper at Cloisterham " (page 34), and " We
cannot suppose that, in the interest of Neville
and Rosa, Grewgious has already sent an
agent to observe Jasper's doings at Cloisterham " (page 35).   To this I venture to reply,
that the very thing I should suppose, from
my estimate of Grewgious's character, and
from his estimate of Jasper's, would be that
Grewgious had already set to work at Cloisterham some time ago.   The mere fact that
Grewgious has not disclosed his plans to
anyone (I think from the evidence afforded by
Chapter xvii, that he did disclose something
to Crisparkle) would not be a sufficient reason
for concluding that he has taken no steps, and
although at the Staple Inn conference he may
not have informed his allies that he had

already made a move, there is every ground
for supposing that as Datchery was his secret
agent, he purposely refrained from taking the
others into his confidence, in the same way
as they refrained from communicating their
intentions to Neville. It may be the fact
that Grewgious had not moved, prior to
July 4th, in the interest of Rosa, but I doubt
very much whether the same could be said as
regards the interest of Neville, and I am firmly
convinced that Grewgious's suspicions of Jasper
would not have permitted him to abstain from
all steps to discover the truth about the murder
until after the date of the chance conference
at Staple Inn. For this reason I demur to
Dr Jackson's conclusion that the conference
was the occasion and the origin of Datchery's
appearance at Cloisterham, and I also demur
to his other conclusion that Dickens's mis-
givings expressed to his sister-in-law were
caused by the discovery that the introduction
of Datchery was premature by five days. Not
only do I think that it was not premature,
but I have very grave doubts indeed whether
Dickens had ever worked out any consistent time-table, such as Dr Jackson has so

ingeniously deduced from the text.   If he had,
however, and if Dr Jackson's chronological
hypothesis were correct, Dickens would have
perceived his error immediately on reading
the proofs, and in lieu of making important
textual revisions in Chapter xviii, he would
simply have set his doubts at rest by trans-
ferring that chapter bodily to its proper place.
He did nothing of the sort, but something
totally different, and pointing in a different
direction.   Ergo, Datchery's appearance was
not considered by Dickens to be premature,
and in my opinion, all the edifice which
Dr Jackson erects upon this basis falls to the
ground.

CHAPTER II

HAVING now, as I believe, obtained some idea of Dickens's main plot, let us see whether it is possible to unravel some of the other mysteries.

First as regards Datchery.

The theory that "Datchery" is Helena Landless, which is now largely meeting with acceptance, appears to me to offer very considerable difficulties from various points of view. Provisionally, these may roughly be classed as follows : (*a*) appearance ; (*b*) time ; (*c*) speech ; but I do not pretend that this classification is exhaustive. However, it will serve for the present.

Let us first take the description of Helena to be found in Chapter VI : " An unusually handsome lithe young fellow, and an unusually handsome lithe girl ; much alike ; *both very dark, and very rich in colour ; she of almost*

3—2

gipsy type; something untamed about them both; a certain air upon them of hunter and huntress; yet withal a certain air of being the objects of the chase, rather than the followers. Slender, supple, quick of eye and limb; half shy, half defiant; *fierce of look*; an indefinable kind of pause coming and going on their whole expression, both of face and form, which might be equally likened to the pause before a crouch or bound." Compare this vivid description with the few lines at the beginning of Chapter XVIII announcing Datchery's appearance: " A white-haired personage, with black eyebrows. Being buttoned up in a *tightish* blue surtout, with *a buff waistcoat* and gray trousers, *he had something of a military air*." A few lines on we find : " This gentleman's head was unusually large, and his shock of white hair was unusually thick and ample. ' I suppose, waiter,' he said, shaking his ' shock of hair' " etc. Upon the strength of the " unusually large head," and upon the strength of that alone, it has been suggested that Datchery was wearing a wig to conceal Helena's " wild black hair " (end of Chapter VII ; note also at the same place the reference to her "lustrous gipsy face" and her "intense dark eyes"), but if Datchery were really wearing a wig, one would hardly expect him to shake his head frequently, for fear of displacing the wig, especially if it were worn over an abundance of natural hair. Later on in the same chapter we find : " Mr Datchery, taking off his hat to give that shock of white hair of his another shake, seemed quite resigned," etc., and yet again, " All this time Mr Datchery had walked with his hat under his arm, and his white hair streaming. He had an odd momentary appearance upon him of having forgotten his hat, when Mr Sapsea now touched it ; and he clapped his hand up to his head as if with some vague expectation of finding another hat upon it. 'Pray be covered, sir,' entreated Mr Sapsea... 'His Honour is very good, but I do it for coolness,' said Mr Datchery." And at the end of the chapter : " Said Mr Datchery to himself that night, as he looked at his white hair," etc., and just previously, "Even then the Worshipper carried his hat under his arm, and gave his streaming white hair to the breeze." I have cited these passages because they may fairly be said to be consistent, in part at least, with Mr Datchery wearing a wig, and the statement in Chapter XXIII " His object in now revisiting his lodging is merely to put on the hat which seems so superfluous an article in his wardrobe" may also be held to support the same view.   (It would be quibbling, I suppose, to suggest that because in this chapter his hair is said to be *grey*, he had *two* wigs.)   I submit, however, that no one assuming the disguise of a wig to escape detection would consist- ently shake his head, or lounge along " with his uncovered gray hair *blowing* about," as Datchery does.   If he really had a thick shock of white hair of his own, the explanation that he goes about with it uncovered " for coolness " is quite reasonable and acceptable ; even the " clapping his hand up to his head, as if with some vague expectation of finding another *hat* upon it " is not conclusive, although, I admit, I have found no suitable explanation of the phrase.   Set against this, however, the constant shaking of the head, and the exposure of the hair to the breeze, as well as to the view (a wig can, I think, be detected by the eye at once) and neither theory will be found to be wholly without objection ; but even a large head and a wig, if admitted, do not make Datchery Helena.

Something has been made of a woman's hands being plump, and easily distinguishable from a man's, and it has been pointed out that Datchery had a habit of putting his hands behind his back. (By the way, Sapsea does this in Chapter XII.) With regard to this point I would suggest, first, that it is distinctly a man's and not a woman's habit, to put his hands behind his back, a habit which he would mechanically adopt even before an empty grate (empty, by the way, because of the season of the year) ; and secondly, that Dickens would hardly have made Datchery hide his hands unless special attention were to be called at some time to the difference between a man's and a woman's hands, which seems quite unlikely. Add to this, also, first, that Datchery wears a buff waistcoat, and secondly, that he lounges about with his hands in his trousers pockets, and thirdly, that he is buttoned up in a tightish blue surtout, all of which facts distinctly prove that he took no pains to conceal his figure, which,

had he been Helena, would have been his first
and constant thought. Further, note his
" something of a military air," and consider
also this sentence, which occurs in Datchery's
interview with the opium woman : " Or, he
suggests, *with a backward hitch of his head,*
you can go up at once," etc. ; to me, it seems
almost impossible to conceive of Helena employing a gesture of this nature. It is hardly
necessary to refer to the fried sole, veal cutlet,
and pint of sherry mentioned in Chapter
XVIII, as constituting Datchery's dinner,
although the sherry appears to be a rather
" large order " for a girl of twenty-one ; admittedly, it might have been ordered to keep up
appearances, and it was not necessary for her
to drink it all. But the ale for supper in the
last chapter can hardly be explained away in
the same manner, nor do I think that Mrs
Tope would long have been in doubt as to the
sex of her lodger. It is unfortunate that we
have no fuller description of the personal
appearance of Datchery than is afforded by
the few lines at the beginning of Chapter
XVIII, but so far as we have one at all, it
differs in every possible detail (except the

black eyebrows) from the detailed description
of Helena already quoted ; and if Helena
could wear a wig, in order to disguise herself,
surely she could also dye her eyebrows !

There are other points referring indirectly
to appearance ; first, Helena was known to all
the inmates of Miss Twinkleton's school ;
secondly (see Chapter xvii), " She has won
her way through those (*i.e.* Cloisterham) streets
until she passes along them as high in the general respect as any one who treads them " ;
thirdly, she had met Jasper at Crisparkle's,
both having been present at the dinner described in Chapter vi, and he had "thanked
her for her vindication of his character."
Contrast with these facts these others ; Helena
disguised as Datchery, relies upon the concealment afforded by a wig and male attire ;
she calls upon Jasper to ask for Tope's character, and assumes that the former, a musician
with a trained ear, capable of identifying a
key by its note, will not recognise her voice ;
she wanders aimlessly about Cloisterham,
where she is well known and respected, with
her striking face undisguised except for a wig
over her hair ; and she carefully keeps the

door of her lodgings open, so that every passer-by, and especially Jasper, may see her. Surely this young lady of twenty-one must have incredible power of self-control and a wonderful capacity for disguising, at the same time as exposing, her face, form, and voice, if she is able thus to meet her former acquaintances at any and every moment without any fear of detection !   Frankly, Dickens would be underrating the perspicacity of his readers if he ever expected them to swallow *this* version of the " Datchery assumption."

My next point has reference to the time of Datchery's appearance on the scene.   We know from Chapter xvii that " Full half a year had come and gone " since the Christmas Eve of Chapter xiv, and " At about this time a stranger appeared at Cloisterham " (Chapter xviii).   That takes us up to about July or August at the latest, but probably not later than July.   Dickens himself transposed Chapters xviii and xix to their present sequence, and apparently regarded the transposition as immaterial.   In Chapter xix we are told " Again Miss Twinkleton has delivered her valedictory address...and again the young ladies have

departed to their several homes. Helena
Landless has left the Nuns' House to attend
her brother's fortunes, and pretty Rosa is
alone." Then follows the interview with
Jasper, and in Chapter xx comes Rosa's
flight ; Helena had evidently been at Miss
Twinkleton's until the end of the term, because " Rosa's mind throughout the last *six
months* had been stormily confused.... She had
been Helena's stay and comfort *during the
whole time*." Further, after the statement at
the beginning of Chapter xvii " Full half a
year had come and gone," we find Crisparkle
telling Neville : " Next week you will cease to
be alone, and will have a devoted companion,"
i.e. Helena. Now, Helena is in London when
Rosa leaves Cloisterham, and yet, by Dickens's
own transposition, the appearance at Cloisterham of Datchery is sandwiched in between
Crisparkle's statement " Next week you will
cease to be alone," and Miss Twinkleton's
breaking-up. If the present order of the chapters can be taken as a guide for the sequence
of the events, Datchery's appearance at
Cloisterham *antedates* Helena's departure. I
admit however that the chronology is hardly

sufficiently definite to allow of any strong argument being based thereon, but if Helena were destined to be her brother's companion and pattern at Staple Inn, it seems at least odd that she is also to keep watch on Jasper at Cloisterham.   Note also what Crisparkle says in Chapter xvii in announcing her arrival, in answer to Neville's objection : " This seems an uncongenial place to bring my sister to." " I don't think so.   There is duty to be done *here* ; and there are *womanly* feeling, sense, and courage wanted *here*."   " I meant," explained Neville, " that the surroundings are so dull and unwomanly, and that Helena can have no suitable friend or society here." " You have only to remember," said Mr Crisparkle, " that you are here yourself, and that she has to draw you into the sunlight."   (I fancy that Crisparkle, if not in the secret, would not have had much difficulty in recognising Helena in Datchery, notwithstanding the disguise of a wig !)

In Chapter xxii we find Rosa taking Billickin's apartments for a *month*, and at the end of that chapter we are told that " the days crept on, and nothing happened."   In Chapter

XXIII, where the story is said to be "above six months old," Jasper comes to London, and is traced to Cloisterham by the opium woman, who meets Datchery there, so that although probably less than a month has elapsed since Helena left Cloisterham to be her brother's companion, she is loitering about in that town, and has been doing so for some time, if she is Datchery. Note in this connexion Datchery's conversation with Deputy: "Halloa, Winks!" "Halloa Dick!" Their acquaintance having seemingly been established on a familiar footing...." We two are good friends, eh, Deputy....Many of my sixpences have come your way since." Helena, if she had ostensibly been in London with her brother, must have made a considerable number of journeys to Cloisterham surreptitiously to arrive at this degree of familiarity with Deputy; her companionship with Neville must have been nominal only. Further, imagine the ingenuity of a striking-looking young lady "unacquainted with all accomplishments, sensitively conscious that I have everything to learn, and deeply ashamed to own my ignorance" as she admits in Chapter

VII, disguising herself almost daily in a wig
and her own eyebrows, and constantly court-
ing, and as constantly evading, detection by
the greatest enemy of her twin brother (whom
she strongly resembles) and her own lover,
under whose nose she lounges about with her
hands in her trousers pockets, without a falter,
and without a blush ! It is useless to suggest
that the Minor Canon was in the secret, for he
had specifically told Neville that " in a week
he would have a devoted companion," and he
was too upright a man to swerve one hairs-
breadth from the truth. The chronological
argument, however, is not strong ; all that
one can say definitely is that Datchery's
appearance is chronicled in Chapter XVIII,
Miss Twinkleton's breaking-up and Helena's
departure " to attend her brother's fortunes "
in Chapter XIX, and Rosa's meeting with
Helena in London in Chapter XXI. I think in
fairness I ought to add that Grewgious's
answer to Rosa's enquiry in Chapter XX (" I
may go to Helena to-morrow ? " " I should
like to sleep on that question to-night ")
might be held to indicate that Helena was not
immediately available, but the plain answer

to that appears to be that she *does* see her, and quite early the next morning, and unless Helena had come to London with Crisparkle by " the very first train to be caught in the morning," she could not have been interviewed by Rosa within the next half-hour, and have been surprised, as she was, to see her in London. Further, the reason for Grewgious's indecision is made apparent in the following chapter.

My third objection, and I think by far the strongest, is the absolute impossibility of Helena talking as Datchery is made to talk. The whole of his conversation with the waiter in Chapter XVIII is inconceivable in the mouth of Helena ; besides, Helena must have known the way to the Cathedral, and probably knew Tope, the verger. The few words Datchery addresses to Jasper are equally impossible of utterance by a young and inexperienced girl, but when we arrive at the somewhat more lengthy conversation with Sapsea, whom Datchery sums up at a glance, I submit that by no means on earth could Helena ever have acquired the knowledge necessary to address him as Datchery addresses him. " The

Worshipful the Mayor," " His Honour," " His Honour the Mayor," these modes of address, and the " third person style of being spoken to," could not by any possibility have been known to Helena, a young girl without any experience of the world, and conscious and ashamed of her own ignorance. And then when Sapsea remarks, " Justice...must be immorally certain—legally, that is," Datchery answers " His Honour reminds me of the nature of the law. Immoral. How true " ; Helena would have been about as likely to twist Sapsea's absurd statement in this way as, say, Crisparkle or Honeythunder. It is noticeable that while Dickens cut out this part of the conversation, he retained the earlier portion, including the peculiar mode of address to which I have called attention. Again, take the whole of Datchery's conversation with the opium woman : " What's his name, deary ? " " Surname, Jasper, Christian name, John. Mr John Jasper." (Would Helena ever have dreamt of phrasing it that way ?) " Has he a calling, good gentleman ? " " Calling ? Yes. Sings in the choir "....
" That's the answer. Go in there at seven

to-morrow morning, and you may see Mr John Jasper, and hear him too ".... " You can admire him at a distance three times a day, whenever you like. *It's a long way to come for that, though.*" Fancy an ignorant, uneducated girl evolving such a neat fishing statement as that ! And then later : " Been here often, *my good woman ?*...Wasn't it a little *cool* to name your sum ? " It seems to me only necessary to contrast these colloquialisms with Helena's conversation to see at once that they were entirely beyond her. And who can imagine Helena saying, in the privacy of her own room : " I like the old *tavern* way of keeping scores. Illegible, except to the scorer. The scorer not committed, the scored *debited* with what is against him. Hum, ha. A very small score this ; a very poor score." Helena was about as likely to know anything of tavern scores, and the old method of keeping them, as the Dean ; probably less. And finally, Datchery accosts the opium woman with " Well, *mistress*," a style of address which I am sure no woman would ever think of adopting to another. If anyone who reads these conversations of Datchery's carefully,

can then support the view that Helena is
speaking, I can only suggest that he must
have a poor opinion of Dickens's power of
differentiation of character ; to me the " most
brilliant literary identification " seems utterly
without foundation, and I think it would
never have been put forward except for the
view that Datchery *must* be a character whose
acquaintance we have already made.

But for the fact that the Helena-Datchery
theory has gained the support of Sir W.
Robertson Nicoll, I should be inclined to
dismiss it without further consideration as
utterly untenable, but his weighty authority
certainly demands that it should be treated
with more respect, and I therefore propose to
examine very shortly the arguments he advances in support.

He starts with the assumption that Datchery was disguised, a fact which, according
to him, is universally admitted. I have
already dealt with Datchery's wig, and have
shown that there are at least some valid
arguments in support of the view that it was
non-existent. I do not propose to reiterate
them, and provisionally, although without

prejudice, as the lawyers say, I will admit the wig.

He next deals with the principles and limitations of disguise, showing by an authority which I am not concerned to question, that there are certain fundamental things which can never be imitated, such as courage or enthusiasm (I do not admit humility), cleverness and truth. Such a proposition is undoubtedly true, and I assent to it unconditionally, but I think it is fatal to our theory, inasmuch as cleverness, adaptability, experience, and knowledge of the world, were just the things which admittedly Helena had *not*, and which Datchery *had*. Daring she may have been, and earnest, but there is absolutely nothing to indicate that she was mentally alert. On the other hand, there was " something untamed" about her, a certain air of huntress, yet withal a certain air of being the object of the chase ; if Crisparkle noticed this on the occasion of their first meeting, it seems hardly likely that within a few months all traces of it should have vanished, and that she would be " lounging along, like the chartered bore of the city." Even the " masterful

look," the "resolution and power" which
Sir W. R. Nicoll calls attention to, seem to
me to refuse to square with Datchery's genial
and brisk character, and I cannot imagine
Helena becoming ecstatic over Mrs Sapsea's
monument in order to ingratiate herself with
the Mayor. And as for describing herself as
a "diplomatic bird," that, I fancy, was a
material and moral impossibility.

I admit the weight of Neville's statement
that when he and Helena ran away, "each
time she dressed as a boy, and showed the
daring of a man," and to my mind it affords
almost the only serious argument in favour of
the Helena-Datchery theory. But I am inclined to think that too much stress can be
laid upon it, in the same way as too much
importance can be attached to Grewgious's
statement concerning Bazzard that "he is
off duty here, altogether, for the present."
Both, I fancy, are false leads, because both are
too obvious to escape attention, and, so far as
I am aware, it was not Dickens's habit to give
direct clues of this nature. I do not suggest, by
the way, that Dickens did not mean his readers
to infer anything from Neville's reference

to Helena's courage, or from her obvious
distrust and dislike of Jasper, but it is not
necessary to assume that the qualities to
which Dickens drew attention could only be
justified if Helena were Datchery, or that he
had not designed to depict a scene where
Jasper, in his pursuit of Rosa, was to be
defied by Helena. By way of a digression, I
think it was not for nothing that the Billickin
was a relative of Bazzard, that she had an
unoccupied third floor, that Rosa went to
lodge with her, and that Bazzard, as I hope to
show, was to play the part of a traitor. I
suggest for consideration the possibility of
Bazzard learning of Rosa's hiding place, and
forthwith revealing it to Jasper ; of the latter
engaging the Billickin's third floor with the
object of meeting Rosa and terrifying her ;
and of Helena getting to hear of his persecu-
tion of Rosa, and straightway bearding Jasper
in his new lodgings and defying him while
protecting Rosa. Surely Helena would have
needed all the courage and resolution, and also
all the hatred and distrust of Jasper, upon
which Sir W. R. Nicoll lays such stress, if
Dickens had meant her to play such a part,

and I fail to discover any reason why the Billickin and Bazzard were related, if Dickens had not had some such intention in view as I have ascribed to him.

I do not at all question that Helena loved Rosa and her brother, and that she probably hated, distrusted, and perhaps suspected Jasper, but I hold that these were qualifications which rather unfitted her for the task of watching Jasper, because love and hate do not conduce to clearness of perception and coolness of action, but rather tend to obscure the one and to prohibit the other. What Datchery needed and had, essentially, was a clear, logical mind, a knowledge of men and the world, perhaps experience of criminals and their ways, and certainly an adaptability of character such as to enable him to consort on terms of equality with all men. That Grewgious, with his practical, matter-of-fact habits, would ever have consented to Helena assuming the task of watching Jasper, seems to me to be quite incomprehensible, and I am of opinion that the Minor Canon would also never have been an assenting party to such an arrangement, not only because it would have shocked his sense of propriety, but also because he would have had legitimate fears for Helena's safety. What she might have dared, he would certainly not have permitted. I have already drawn attention to the fact that it was Crisparkle who announced to Neville that his sister was shortly coming to London to be his companion, and seeing that he and Grewgious were secretly working the case together (see the beginning of Chapter XXI, where Grewgious says of Crisparkle " And it was particularly kind of him to come, for he had but just gone ") I can only conclude that he knew exactly what was going on, so that his statement to Neville must be accepted literally, if he is not to be held guilty of a wilful and unnecessary falsehood.

The argument drawn from the long passage in Chapter XVII which Dickens deleted, does not appear on consideration to merit great weight, for Dickens allowed to stand the short but important phrase in which Crisparkle announced Helena's arrival. What he excised had reference partly to the reasons for Helena being required in London, partly to Crisparkle's eulogy of Helena's character.

That he struck out the one and retained the other, seems to go to prove, not what Sir W. R. Nicoll wants it to prove, but the exact contrary.

Datchery's " wistful gaze " I am unable to explain satisfactorily, but neither can I explain Helena's " wistful gaze," nor do I think Sir W. R. Nicoll has done so. " Wistful " is hardly an epithet which fits Helena in any circumstances, and the context does not, I think, warrant his interpretation of the whole phrase. " As mariners on a dangerous voyage, *approaching an iron-bound coast* may look along the beams of the warning light to the haven lying beyond it *that may never be reached*, so Mr Datchery's wistful gaze is directed to this beacon, and *beyond*." So far as it is possible to interpret this enigmatic sentence, I should feel inclined to consider that it had reference to Datchery's knowledge of the difficulty and danger of his task, especially at that juncture, and to his desire to unravel an apparently insoluble mystery, but the allusion offers immense difficulties unless we can show that Datchery did have, as Sir W. R. Nicoll urges, some personal interest in tracking Jasper. Of this, later on.

As regards Datchery's hands, if he had really wanted to conceal them, he might have worn a pair of gloves, but I think the point is a very weak one, because, as I have shown, Datchery seems to have taken no real pains to conceal his figure. Further, I doubt seriously whether Helena would have troubled to conceal her hands from a waiter, or even from the opium woman, and she would certainly have required her hands to copy the inscription on Mrs Sapsea's monument, the opportunity for transcribing which might well have been deferred, as Dickens himself pointed out. If Datchery's hands are clasped behind him or are in his trousers pockets during his walk with the opium woman, it is, in the one case, because he is "lounging," and in the other, because he is rattling his money, and tempting her to speak.

Sir W. R. Nicoll argues that Datchery did not stretch out his hand for his hat at the "Crozier" because he was afraid that the waiter would notice its shape; without suggesting that so observant a man would have been wasted as a waiter, is it not permissible to suppose that the hat was some distance off ? Again, we are told that Datchery does not shake hands with Jasper or the Mayor; neither does Edwin with Grewgious, nor Crisparkle with Honeythunder. We are asked to assume (because we are nowhere told it as a fact) that, because Datchery carried his hat under his arm, one hand would be buried in it; I do not think the inference is a legitimate one, in fact, I should be inclined to infer that by carrying his hat under his arm, Datchery had both hands free. Coming to his interview with the opium woman, we are asked to draw an important conclusion from the fact that Dickens originally wrote " greedily watching *him* " and subsequently altered the phrase to " greedily watching his *hands*." But as Datchery was counting out money to give to the woman, surely the most natural thing for her to do was to watch *the hands* with which he was counting it; and if, while he was counting out money to give to her, she had watched *him* and not *his hands* containing the money, would that not have been more remarkable, without taking into consideration the adjective " greedily " ? Then, Datchery drops some money, and stoops to pick it up;

Sir W. R. Nicoll would have us believe that if Datchery, after *slowly* counting out " the sum demanded of him," finding he has counted wrong, shaking his money together, and beginning again, drops some money and stoops to pick it up, it is because he suspects his hands are being watched. But the real reason was that he heard, for the first time, that the " young gentleman's name was Edwin." And so possessed is Sir W. R. Nicoll by the theory, that while he argues that this infirm and greedy old woman, waiting eagerly for alms, nevertheless had sufficient detachment of mind to consider Datchery's hands, he seriously advances the view that Jasper, with his trained musician's ear, consumed as he was with hatred and jealousy of Neville, failed to recognise the voice or face of Helena, Neville's striking-looking twin sister ! This, it appears to me, is not criticism, but prepossession.

Even the suggested origin of Dickens's idea is without any real bearing on the point ; for, as regards the figure in real life, the impersonation by a girl of a male character for a couple of hours on the stage is essentially different, as Dickens would have known, from its permanent assumption in real life, while the example quoted from fiction (Wilkie Collins's *No Name*) is a mere general statement, in fiction, and without authority.

So far as Dickens's excisions from the proofs are concerned, I propose to deal with them later under another heading; for the present I need only say that they appear to me to afford no support whatever to the Helena-Datchery theory.

Sir W. R. Nicoll remarks that the idea that Datchery is a new character may safely be dismissed, and that it is in one of the characters already on the stage that we must find him. I have carefully searched his book in order to ascertain upon what grounds he bases this assertion, and I can find two reasons only : the first is contained in his chapter entitled "The Methods of Dickens," and the second is stated in the following words : " I have taken no account of the theory that Datchery is an unknown person. An unknown person could not possess the necessary qualities of heart." This second reason, in my opinion, really begs the question, inasmuch as if

Datchery were not one of the characters
already known, he might still turn out to be
some one with a direct and strong interest in
either Rosa or Edwin. This would be quite in
keeping with Dickens's methods, and I shall
deal with the point when stating my own views
as to Datchery's identity. As regards the first
ground, I need only point out that Datchery
is introduced at the beginning of Chapter XVIII,
a little more than one-third of the book as
planned, so that we are well within the limit
set by Sir W. R. Nicoll himself for the introduction of important new characters. In
" Bleak House," for example, Mr Bucket
appears in Chapter XXII, and several important characters appear considerably later. In
" Our Mutual Friend " every character of
significance has been introduced, says Sir
W. R. Nicoll, when the first half ends, and the
same remark applies to " Little Dorrit."
" Thus," he states, " we may say, taking the
three long books of Dickens's later period, that
in each it was his manner to introduce no
new character of the least import in the *second*
half of the book." Admitting, for the sake
of argument, that this view is accurate, how

does it militate in the least against the contention that Datchery is a new character,
seeing that he is introduced at the beginning
of Chapter xviii, while the book was apparently planned to have some 48 or 50 chapters ?
From another point of view, Chapter xviii
was (if the monthly parts were of equal length)
the second chapter in part Five ; Datchery is
thus well on the scene within Sir W. R. Nicoll's
limit, and he re-appears in Chapter xxiii,
which is also not quite half way through the
book.   Either, therefore, I have quite mis-
understood the argument, or it is not adapted
to support the superstructure reared upon it ;
as I have read and re-read the chapter of
Sir W. R. Nicoll's book to which I have
referred without being able to give it any
other interpretation than that stated above, I
am obliged to adopt the second alternative.

Dr Henry Jackson, who accepts the Helena-
Datchery theory, apparently for want of a
better one, largely bases his conclusions upon
two facts, namely, the alleged proper sequence
of the chapters, and Helena's suggestion that it
would be advisable to try and anticipate any
further pursuing and maligning of Neville on

the part of Jasper, which he considers to be
the origin of Datchery's employment. He
is a scrupulously fair controversialist, and is
as ready to state any points which seemingly
militate against the view he advocates as those
which appear to support it. Thus, he admits
that while his theory would logically call for
the placing of Chapter XVIII after Chapter
XXII, what Dickens did was to put it into the
place it now occupies in lieu of the present
Chapter XIX, so that instead of being transposed to a *later* position, it actually occupies
an earlier one than Dickens originally planned.
This fact in itself, candidly admitted by
Dr Jackson, should, I imagine, have caused
him to consider seriously whether, after all,
the arrangement adopted by Dickens was
not the one which he felt to be best calculated to contribute to the continuity of
his story, and personally I feel quite convinced
that the transposition of Chapters XVIII and
XIX, after a few pages only of the former had
been written, must be accepted as clear proof
that, in Dickens's view at least, there was
nothing incongruous in making Datchery
appear on the scene at the period assigned to

him by the present sequence of the chapters. Dickens himself corrected the proofs up to and including Chapter XXI, so that he had ample opportunity, if he had so desired, of removing Chapter XVIII from its present place, and putting it where, according to Dr Jackson, it should have appeared if his view is correct. Consequently, I can only conclude that Dickens experienced no difficulty or doubt whatever with reference to the *time* of Datchery's appearance. The doubts which he expressed to Miss Hogarth had reference, in my opinion, not to the period of Datchery's introduction, but to what Dickens had originally told the reader about Datchery's enquiries concerning the murder of Drood; that this is so may, I believe, be safely inferred from the fact that Dickens subsequently deleted all passages in Chapter XVIII directly or indirectly indicating that Datchery was in any way concerned about the tragedy. It is interesting to note, in this connexion, that whereas Proctor wrote (*Knowledge*, November, 1887) " Dickens did, indeed, express to Miss Hogarth the fear that the Datchery assumption had been so handled in the last

chapter (written) as to disclose too much,"
Sir W. R. Nicoll says, at page 171 of his book,
" We know that Dickens told his sister-in-law
that he was afraid the Datchery assumption
in the *fifth number* was premature." I am
not aware where either of these writers got
his information from, nor can I judge between
them as to the accuracy of their several statements, but if it is legitimate to draw an inference from the alterations actually made by
Dickens, we are led to the conclusion that
neither statement is strictly correct, and I
prefer, with great deference to the views of
these two authorities, to interpret the doubts
which Dickens certainly did express, by reference to the alterations which he as certainly
made. I hold, therefore, notwithstanding
Dr Jackson's interesting and closely reasoned
argument, that Chapter XVIII is in its proper
position, and that we must take it as we find
it, with all the consequences which it entails.
I have not overlooked the fact that there is no
obvious connexion between Datchery's doings,
as related in Chapter XVIII, with the events
recorded in Chapter XVII, and Chapters XIX
to XXII, but to this I reply, first, that it was

Dickens's habit to keep all the threads of his story going at the same time, which necessitated a certain apparent want of continuity between the consecutive chapters ; and secondly, that if Chapter xviii were transposed to a position after Chapter xxii, we should see a great deal of Datchery in two consecutive chapters, very much to the detriment of the interest in the other characters.　Further, it is quite plain from the conversation between Datchery and Deputy that the former had, at the period of the events narrated in Chapter xxiii, been in Cloisterham for some relatively considerable time, so that the further back we put Datchery's appearance, the better we explain their close acquaintance.

Another argument relied upon by Dr Jackson is, I think, really based upon the statement made by Grewgious about Crisparkle at the beginning of Chapter xxi, " And it was particularly kind of him to come, for he had but just gone." He infers from this that Crisparkle's visit must be that chronicled in Chapter xvii, no other being mentioned in the intervening chapters ; that was, according to Dr Jackson's chronology, on June 30th, and as the Staple Inn conference did not take place until July 4th, before which date the allies had apparently not planned to have Jasper watched at Cloisterham, Datchery's appearance there on June 30th or July 1st as their agent, is totally inexplicable. He regards it as impossible that Grewgious had already set a watch on Jasper in the interests of Rosa or Neville, as at the conference on July 4th their defence is discussed as a *res integra*; before this date, therefore, Grewgious and his friends can hardly have taken the field, either offensively, with a view to discovering the murderer of Edwin, or defensively, with a view to the protection of Neville and Rosa. " In a word," he argues, " Datchery seems to be a representative or agent of the Staple Inn allies ; but it is inconceivable that they should have had a representative or agent at Cloisterham on Friday, June 30th, or Saturday, July 1st. On the other hand, the appearance of such a representative or agent on any day subsequent to the Staple Inn conference, say on July 5th or July 6th, is exactly what we should expect." " Let us suppose," he continues later on, " that while

Tartar will get into touch with Jasper when he visits Staple Inn, Datchery, whoever he may be, is to observe Jasper's movements when he is at Cloisterham.   This is an intelligible scheme, whereas the conference is strangely ineffective if its sole result is that Tartar is told off to verify Crisparkle's conjectural explanation of Jasper's visits to Staple Inn, especially as that explanation has now been justified by Jasper's words to Rosa."

" If, therefore," he concludes, " about this time " means July 5th, it follows that Chapter XVIII *must* come after Chapter XXII.

It appears to me, if I have correctly followed Dr Jackson's argument (and I trust that in summarising it I have not involuntarily done it injustice) that it depends very largely upon the identification of the visit of Crisparkle referred to in Chapter XXI with that mentioned in Chapter XVII, for if " About this time " does not mean June 30th, it might mean practically any other date, whether a week or a month previously.   Now, I cannot admit that if Crisparkle had not seen Grewgious later than June 30th, the latter could have fairly said on July 4th " He had *only just* gone " ; he might have said " He was here a few days ago " or " last week," but he could not justify " only just gone." I argue, therefore, that Grewgious and Crisparkle had seen one another recently, and had, in fact, been conferring for some time past as to the best method of bringing Jasper to justice, and I can see nothing unlikely in a watch having been set on Jasper some time previously, either by Grewgious alone, or by him in agreement with Crisparkle. Grewgious " had reason to know that a local friend of ours sneaks to and fro, and dodges up and down " ; that at least shows that he had had Jasper under observation for some time, either privately or in conjunction with Crisparkle. We know, in fact, that Grewgious himself was watching Jasper at Staple Inn, and that Bazzard was off duty there entirely at that time. But unless Grewgious had some watcher at Cloisterham, it is difficult to see how he could have learned of this " sneaking to and fro and dodging up and down," and this knowledge appears to be consistent only with the presence at Cloisterham of some agent or representative who transmitted information to him of Jasper's movements. *Prima facie*, therefore, there is every reason to think that on July 4th, the date of the " conference," Grewgious had on his own account an observer at Cloisterham, and in the circumstances this could be none other than Datchery, and he must have been there for some time to warrant Grewgious speaking as he did. Instead, therefore, of placing Datchery's appearance at Cloisterham *later* than July 4th, I should feel inclined to put it earlier than June 30th.

With regard to the " ineffective " conference, let me observe that it was a perfectly accidental one, so that one would hardly expect any concerted plan to be evolved. Rosa flies to London, and takes refuge with Grewgious; Crisparkle follows the next day, because Miss Twinkleton was so uneasy; Tartar recognises him, and, with apologies, makes one of the company; and then Mr Grewgious suddenly has an idea, whereby Rosa and Helena can meet without Jasper's spy being any the wiser. The only suggestion of a scheme comes from Helena, and all that she proposes, is that Tartar should visit Neville, so that if Jasper should communicate with Tartar, " we might not only know the fact, but might know from Mr Tartar what the terms of the communication were." That, I take it, is the extent of her plan to " anticipate" Jasper, and the conference, having come together fortuitously, and without any pre-arranged idea of formulating any scheme, breaks up when Helena's proposal is carried.

But even if we assume that all my arguments are wrong, that Grewgious had no agent at Cloisterham before the date of the conference, that Datchery only goes there after July 4th, that Dr Jackson's suggested chronology is accurate, and that Chapter xviii was designed to follow Chapter xxii, then I would still maintain that Helena could not have been Datchery, if Dickens was dealing fairly with his readers, for the following reason. The fourth paragraph of Chapter xxiii runs as follows : " The dreadful suspicion of Jasper, which Rosa was so shocked to have received into her imagination, appeared to have no harbour in Mr Crisparkle's. If it ever haunted *Helena's* thoughts or Neville's, neither gave it one spoken word of utterance." The clear suggestion conveyed by this last

sentence can only be that Helena, as well as
Neville, was available to all their friends, and
if Dickens had ever intended that his readers
were to be told that Helena was to have been
shown to have been at Cloisterham when they
had every right to infer that she was at Staple
Inn, he would have been the first to admit
that the words quoted above were grossly and
unfairly misleading. He was not obliged, in
the paragraph under consideration, to make
any reference at all to Helena ; no one could
have complained of the omission had he left
out her name entirely, and probably no one
would have noticed it. If Helena were Datchery, assuredly Dickens would never have
written the words quoted ; that he did so
amounts, in my opinion, to clear and absolute
proof that, whoever Datchery was, he was
not Helena.

I think that this reference in Chapter XXIII
to Helena partly meets Mr J. Cuming Walters's
point that we hear no more of her after
Datchery comes on the scene ; the reference
to her is not, indeed, a very definite one, but
it is enough to prove that Dickens was not
hiding Helena. The argument that she does

not call on Rosa carries no weight with me,
as we know that Jasper was watching Neville's
chambers ; had Helena visited Rosa, the spy,
in following her, would have located Rosa,
Jasper would have learnt of her address, and
all the elaborate precautions taken by Grewgious for Rosa's protection would have been
nullified.

Apparently, also, neither Grewgious nor
Crisparkle nor even Tartar visits Rosa, although Tartar was to serve as a medium of
communication between Rosa and Helena.
Mr Walters's argument, therefore, either proves
too much or proves nothing at all, and by
reason of the fact that Tartar and Rosa were
definitely intended to meet, although we are
never told that they did, I conclude that
nothing can be inferred from Dickens's omission to tell us whether Helena called on Rosa.
However far-seeing Dickens may have been,
he could not possibly have anticipated how a
mere omission might be tortured into evidence
in favour of a " mystery " which, in all
probability, he never had in his mind.

If Datchery is not Helena, is he Bazzard
or Drood ? I think neither the one nor the

other. Bazzard is a surly sulky brute in
character, entirely unlike brisk and cheery
Datchery. He has his " mystery," but it is
not the Datchery mystery. In appearance,
he is a " pale, puffy-faced dark-haired person
of thirty, with big dark eyes that wholly
wanted lustre, and a dissatisfied doughy
countenance that seemed to ask to be sent to
the baker's ; a gloomy person with tangled
locks." The one thing that Datchery is *not*,
is gloomy ; and imagine Datchery speaking
thus : " Mr Drood," said Bazzard. " What
of him ? " " Has called," said Bazzard.
" You might have shown him in." " I am
doing it," said Bazzard. Or again : " Dine
presently with Mr Drood and me." " If I'm
ordered to dine of course I will, sir," was the
gloomy answer. " Save the man ; you're
not ordered, you're invited." " Thank you,
sir ; in that case I don't care if I do." It
seems useless to pursue the Bazzard theory
any further ; it is only built upon Grewgious's
statement to Rosa " he is off duty here, altogether, just at present," and has no other
shred of evidence in its favour. If Dickens
designed to make Bazzard Datchery, he simply

did not know his business. Besides, I think
I can provide Bazzard with another rôle, and
an important one.

As regards the Drood theory, the internal
evidence is not so decisive, but I refer again
to the interview between Datchery and Sapsea, and ask, whether a young man of twenty-
one, who admitted that he was not clever,
was likely to know or adopt the style of
address used by Datchery ? I think the
probabilities are all against such a view.
Datchery was certainly bright and cheery,
but he quite evidently had not the " giddy
head " ascribed to Edwin in Chapter ɪɪ ; he
had a much older and clearer head than Edwin
would have possessed for many years, and a
manner of adapting his conversation to the
person he was addressing, which Drood certainly had not, as witness the latter's interview with Grewgious. And then, think of
the utter impossibility of Jasper, Edwin's
uncle, companion, and rival, and Mrs Tope,
whom he had joked with and kissed, failing to
recognise him because he happens to wear a
wig ! Two things are very difficult to disguise,
the eyes, and the voice, the latter especially ;

Jasper was a sufficiently keen musician to be able to discriminate between and identify three keys by their respective notes, and Dickens makes it clear that his sense of sound was highly developed, and it accordingly appears to me incredible that he could for a moment have imagined that Datchery, if he were Drood, would have risked, or could have hoped to escape, detection by Jasper, under any disguise whatever. Jasper is the first person, after Mrs Tope, whom Datchery visits at Cloisterham ; neither of them has the slightest suspicion of ever having seen him before, although he has a moderately lengthy conversation with each of them. Mrs Tope waits on him, prepares his meals, attends to his wants, and probably sees him every day of his life ; Jasper no doubt passes him daily at his open door, and meets him " lounging " about the cathedral precincts. But neither of them recognises or even suspects him ; the wonderful wig does the trick ! With the greatest respect for the memory of the late Mr R. A. Proctor, who, I think, started the Drood theory, I cannot believe that Dickens would ever have required his

readers to swallow such a host of incon-
sistencies as are involved in the identification
of Drood with Datchery.

In my opinion, however, the interview
between Datchery and the opium woman is
decisive. Drood had met her on Christmas
Eve ; he had recognised the effects of opium,
and had even asked her whether she ate
opium. She had begged for three-and-six ;
had been told that his name was Edwin ; had
enquired whether the short of that name was
Eddy (*not* Ned, by the way), and whether
sweethearts did not call it so ; finally, she had
informed him that Ned was a threatened
name. When Datchery meets her, he does
not recognise her, or at least shows no signs
of so doing. He asks whether she has been
there often, points out that she knows the way
to the travellers' lodging (which he evidently
knew from Deputy), and evinces no interest
or astonishment when informed that a young
gentleman once gave her three-and-six on
that very spot. Were Edwin Datchery, I
suggest that he could not have helped being
reminded of the events of the preceding Christmas Eve (a somewhat remarkable day for

him), both by the woman's talk, and by her very precise statement, but they both leave him quite cold. When, however, she states that her medicine is opium, "Mr Datchery, with a sudden change of countenance, gives her a sudden look." I take this to mean, that Datchery, up to this point, not being Edwin, certainly had no *precise* knowledge, and probably no knowledge at all, of the meeting between the latter and the woman on Christmas Eve; but that, on hearing the word "opium," he recognises that he may have happened on a likely clue. It is not until she mentions "The young gentleman's name was Edwin" that Mr Datchery, becoming startled at his luck in stumbling upon this witness, drops some money, stoops to pick it up, and reddens with the exertion. "How do you know the young gentleman's name?" enquires he; a perfectly needless and foolish question, by the way, if he were Edwin. And she answers: "I asked him for it, and he told it me." Now Edwin-Datchery would either have recognised the woman directly he met her, or immediately after the three-and-six episode, and he would not have blushed when he heard the name Edwin; that he reddened only at that particular moment, conclusively proves, to my mind, that Datchery is not Edwin.

A further proof that Datchery and Edwin are not one, is to be found in his first conversation with Deputy. " Lookie yonder," says Deputy. " You see that there winder and door ? " " That's Tope's ? " answers Datchery, lying quite needlessly, apparently, if he were Edwin, who knew very well that it wasn't. " Yer lie; it ain't. That's Jarsper's," replies Deputy. " ' Indeed ? ' said Mr Datchery, with a *second look of some interest.*" Dickens deleted these words in the proof, but that only shows that when he wrote them he had not observed that they might serve to narrow down the small number of people who might be Datchery, or that they disclosed some interest in Jasper on the part of Datchery which Dickens desired to hide. Finally, the last words of Chapter xix hardly fit in with the Edwin-Datchery theory, since, except for facing the ordeal of meeting Jasper and Mrs Tope, Edwin's afternoon (if it were he), could hardly be described as *busy.*

It has been suggested that Datchery was Tartar, but I do not think that anything can be said in favour of this theory. The following description of Tartar occurs towards the end of Chapter XVII, " A handsome gentleman, with a young face, but with an older figure in its robustness and its breadth of shoulder ; say a man of eight-and-twenty, or at the utmost thirty ; so extremely sunburnt that the contrast between his brown visage and the white forehead shaded out of doors by his hat, and the glimpses of white throat below the neckerchief, would have been almost ludicrous but for his broad temples, bright blue eyes, clustering brown hair and laughing teeth." Contrast this with the description of Datchery at the beginning of Chapter XVIII, remembering Datchery's habit of dispensing with his hat, and it is at once obvious that Tartar's " white forehead " (which would have been as noticeable as Datchery's " black eyebrows ") would have certainly led him to wear a hat at all times, if he desired to remain unrecognised. There are also very great difficulties connected with his watching Jasper at Cloisterham, at the same time as he was to be in daily communication with Neville in London, and while I agree that Tartar was probably intended to play some part in the unmasking or capture of Jasper, I do not think that anything points to this part being an important one, or one which required the qualities with which Dickens endowed Datchery. A naval lieutenant would have been as incapable as Helena or Edwin of adopting the style of address which Datchery used with Sapsea, and it is quite improbable that he would have been possessed of Datchery's subtlety and irony. Finally, Datchery's settling at Cloisterham does not square with Tartar's appearance on the scene, as we know that the latter went to Staple Inn nine months before Neville, and apparently remained there during the remainder of the story, so far as we have it. Tartar's claim to be Datchery may therefore, I think, be safely dismissed as quite untenable.

Now, if Datchery was neither Edwin, nor Helena, nor Bazzard, nor Tartar, who was he ? I do not admit that the argument is conclusive that the story was in too advanced a stage for a new character to have been introduced, but I agree that, if possible, it would be more satisfactory to identify Datchery with some known personage. That he was a detective in the ordinary sense, and similar to Dickens's other detective characters, is disproved by the internal evidence, as Datchery is an educated gentleman, a very "diplomatic bird," and a kind-hearted man, but that he is obviously doing detective duty is apparent. The problem can be approached, I think, from two directions : first, by looking for some character who has not hitherto been identified with Datchery, and secondly, by searching for corroborative evidence in his speech and habits.

Let us first turn to Chapter xi, where we are told something about Grewgious ; there is a good deal of mystery about his business, which is stated to be that of a Receiver and Agent. The whole paragraph is worth transcribing, after noting that he had been "bred to the Bar." "Coy Conveyancing would not come to Mr Grewgious. She was wooed and not won, and they went their several ways. But an Arbitration being blown towards him by some unaccountable wind, and he gaining great credit for it as one indefatigable in seeking out right and doing right, a pretty fat Receivership was next blown into his pocket by a wind more traceable to its source. So, by chance, he found his niche. Receiver and Agent now, to two rich estates, and deputing their legal business, in an amount worth having, to a firm of solicitors on the floor below, he had snuffed out his ambition...." By way of digression, be it noted that the two rich estates cannot have been Rosa's and Edwin's, as she only had an annuity of £250, and Edwin " would...come into his partnership derived from his father, and into its arrears to his credit (if any) on attaining his majority..."; so Grewgious tells Rosa in Chapter ix. The "unaccountable wind," and the " wind more traceable to its source," and the " two rich estates " hardly appear to me to be mentioned for no purpose whatever, and I believe that they would have had some connexion with the story, although I am at a loss to offer any suggestion. But to revert to our argument. When Rosa visits Grewgious at Staple Inn, he tells her, by way of general conversation, that Bazzard " is off duty here, altogether, just at present ; and a firm downstairs, with which I have business relations, lend me a substitute.'' We thus find that the firm of solicitors, to whom, as we are told, Grewgious *deputed his legal business* in an amount worth having, find him a substitute for the absent Bazzard ; is it impossible that he should also have interested this firm in the enquiries which he has undoubtedly instituted at Cloisterham ? In my view, it is not only not unlikely, but exceedingly probable ; it would have been only natural for Grewgious to turn for aid to his ordinary legal advisers, more particularly as they were unknown to the person to be watched. For no apparent reason, Dickens has twice referred to this firm ; in vague and general words, it is true, but sufficiently definitely to bring out their close connexion with Grewgious. He thus escapes the accusation of having introduced at too late a stage an entirely new character, and at the same time so little, and that little so apparently unimportant, has been said of this character, that, so far as I am aware, the identification with Datchery has never been suggested to this day.

Now, let us see whether Datchery's speech affords any corroboration of his identity with Grewgious's lawyer-friend. First take his interview with Sapsea, noting, by the way, how admirably he adapts his style of address and speech to the solemn jackass, and what different styles he assumes with Deputy and the opium woman respectively; a diplomatic bird, indeed ! Who but a lawyer would ever think of addressing Sapsea as " The Worshipful the Mayor," " His Honour," or " His Honour the Mayor " ? Such a mode of address would, on the other hand, suggest itself *naturally* and almost infallibly to a lawyer desirous of flattering a provincial Mayor, as also would, though perhaps not quite so naturally, the third-person style of address. Even the obtuse Durdles scents the legal flavour in Datchery's style of address. " Who's His Honour ? " asks he. " I was never brought afore him, and it will be time enough for me to ' Honour ' him when I am." And then consider Datchery's confession when Sapsea states, as a general remark, that Diplomacy is a fine profession. " There I confess His Honour the Mayor is too many for me; even a diplomatic bird must fall to such a gun." Without actually asserting a falsehood, Datchery has satisfied the solemn jackass's curiosity by a particularly subtle answer. And then his answer to Sapsea's remark, that "Justice must be immorally certain—legally, that is "; "His Honour reminds me of the nature of the law. Immoral. How true!" Read the whole of this scene aloud to any moderately experienced lawyer, and suggest to him, if he is not beforehand with the suggestion, that Datchery was a member of the legal profession, and I think that in nine cases out of ten the theory will gain his immediate adherence.

If we take the conversation with the opium woman, the impression is strengthened; Datchery is not now flattering a fool, but extracting information from a witness. Having given her Jasper's name, "the burst of triumph in which she thanks him does not escape the attention of the single buffer living idly on his means." He "lounges along the echoing precincts at her side," suggests that she "can go up at once to Mr Jasper's rooms there," and adds "It's a long way to come for that, though," a subtle way

of eliciting information as to where she has
come from. (Edwin knew that she came from
London.) Finding that the fish does not bite,
but still desiring to ascertain what she wants
with Jasper, the man that he is also after,
Datchery lounges along, and tempts her by
rattling the loose money in the pockets of his
trousers. He has accompanied her sufficiently far to note that she is making directly
for the travellers' lodging, or rather he has
made a shot in the dark, as a legal man in
search of information might do. Then still
rattling his money, and still tempting her,
he enquires : "Been here often, my good
woman ? " speaking as any lawyer, examining
a witness of the lower classes, would speak.
Having got her to talk, he lets her talk without interruption until he has heard all she has
to say, delaying payment until it becomes
necessary (it would not have been necessary
for Edwin) to ask : " How do you know the
young gentleman's name ? "; he has a willing
witness, and, as every lawyer knows, it is
wise to let her tell her own tale. Then come
the conversation with Deputy, where Datchery
is short, sharp, and to the point ; the soliloquy,

concerning the old tavern way of keeping
scores, which would commend itself to a
shrewd lawyer; and finally, the last words with
Princess Puffer, all of which appear to me
to be highly characteristic. Add to this the
fried sole, veal cutlet, and pint of sherry, the
bread and cheese and ale, Dickens's legal
experience, and his constant habit of intro-
ducing legal characters into his novels, especially where delicate work is to be done, and I
think that we have ample corroboration of
the theory that Datchery was a member of
the firm of solicitors to whom Grewgious
deputed his legal work, and who found him
a substitute for Bazzard.

The acceptance of this theory renders
unnecessary the presence of Helena in two
places at the same time, and enables us to
acquit the Minor Canon of a falsehood. It also
does away with the necessity of convicting
Dickens of an attempt to make his readers
believe that a wig would effectively disguise
either Helena or Edwin from people who
knew them well. Upon this theory, also,
Dickens may be acquitted of wilfully misleading his readers when he describes how

Datchery becomes bewildered in proceeding
from the Crozier to the Cathedral, in reaching
which neither Edwin nor Helena could have
experienced the slightest difficulty.

The only phrase in the whole book which
does not square with my hypothesis, is Datchery's "wistful gaze" to which reference is made
in Chapter xxiii. It has been pointed out,
and rightly, I think, that the word " wistful "
implies a close personal and affectionate
interest on the part of Datchery in the matter
he is investigating, an interest such as Helena
or Edwin might have had, but which is quite
unlikely in a stranger. I can only reply,
first, that Datchery's gaze is directed " to
this beacon, *and beyond*," whatever that may
imply, and secondly, that it is not certain
that he is only a lawyer, *and nothing else*. We
are told, for example, in Chapter ix, that
" Rosa, having no relation *that she knew of in
the world*, had from the seventh year of her
age, known no home but the Nuns' House."
If Dickens had wanted to say that she *had* no
relations, he would assuredly have said so ;
if he had wanted his readers to *assume* that
she had none, while leaving the door open

for the introduction of one later, he could hardly have chosen a form of words more apt to his purpose. While, therefore, I can offer no definite explanation of the word " wistful" I think I am at least entitled to put forward, as a tentative explanation, the theory that Datchery would have been found to be in some way related to Rosa, and therefore personally interested in Jasper's conviction. The mere use of one doubtful word, cannot, I think, be held to invalidate a theory otherwise quite consistent with all the known facts, more particularly as Dickens did in fact commit one or two errors which are attributable to carelessness. As is well known, he places Rosa's picture in Jasper's lodgings first in the outer room, and afterwards in the inner one ; as I have pointed out, Datchery's hair is white in Chapter XVIII, and grey in Chapter XXIII ; Grewgious is described in Chapter IX as near-sighted, although in Chapter XVII his sight seems particularly good ; finally, I think I shall be able to prove Dickens guilty of a much graver error, which, I believe, has escaped attention altogether until now (unless it be his commentators, and not Dickens, who are at fault).

Upon these grounds, therefore, I think my identification of Datchery is the one which offers the least difficulty, and which can find the soundest arguments in its favour.

CHAPTER III

THE Edwin-Datchery theory of course necessitates acceptance of the view that Edwin was not really killed, but only pretended to be. This particular difficulty is not involved in any other identification of Datchery, although, on the other hand, the view that Drood is dead is not without its own difficulties. Let us, however, first see what reason there is for thinking that he was murdered, and effectually murdered.

In the first place, there is Dickens's own statement to Fildes, to whom he said : " I must have the double neck-tie. It is necessary, for Jasper strangles Drood with it." This is certainly strong evidence, although, be it noted, Dickens eventually gave Jasper a " large black scarf of strong close-woven silk, slung loosely round his neck." He may have done this, however, because Fildes pointed out that Jasper had been depicted with a small tie only, and probably because the scarf seemed to him a more effective weapon.

In the next place, there are Dickens's own notes under the various chapters, two of which at least are most important. Under Chapter II we find the following note : " Uncle and Nephew. Murder very far off," while under Chapter XII there occurs the significant statement : " Lay the ground for the manner of the murder to come out at last." I think that it is indisputable that in these notes, which were written for Dickens's private use and guidance only, and which he did not dream would ever be disclosed, we may look for the plain truth without any concealment or afterthought ; if that is so, we are entitled to assume that at least when they were made, Dickens intended Drood to be murdered. Of course, he may subsequently have changed his mind, and have revised his original plot so as to permit of Edwin being resuscitated, but there is no evidence whatever upon which to base such a theory.

Other notes, such as that to Chapter VII : " Jasper lays his ground " ; to Chapter X :

" Smoothing the way. That is, for Jasper's plan " ; and to Chapter xii : " Jasper's failure in the one great object made known by Grewgious," all tend entirely in the same direction, and unless Dickens meant by the word " murder " in his own notes, merely " attempted murder," we are bound to admit that the evidence in support of Edwin's death which these notes afford is almost irrefutable. The contrary view involves either an unnecessary precaution or a rather silly self-mystification on Dickens's part, or else a sudden change of plot for no apparent reason, and on these grounds alone I should decline to accept it.

Extrinsic evidence in the same sense is also forthcoming from Dickens's son and daughter, which is to be found in Sir W. Robertson Nicoll's book already referred to, and need not therefore be quoted here ; and finally, there is the intrinsic evidence to be gathered from the book itself. In this connexion, the strongest point, I think, is, as numerous writers have remarked, that if Drood were alive, he could hardly have allowed Neville to remain under suspicion merely

in order to inflict a particularly gruesome
form of punishment on Jasper, as Proctor
suggested. Of course, Proctor did not know
of Dickens's notes, and he was not without
justification when he imagined that the ring
was introduced for a particularly dramatic
purpose. With the materials at his disposal,
he could conceive of no other necessity for
Jasper to abstract this ring than with a view
to avoiding identification of the body ; and
for the infliction of the punishment which he
imagined, Edwin had to be alive. Now that
I have shown, as I think, that Jasper had
another object in view, namely, the inculpation of Neville, the dramatic situation which
Proctor imagined could have been brought
about without entailing any necessity for
assuming that Edwin was still alive, and was
heartlessly allowing Neville to remain under
suspicion, and I think that, in the circumstances, Proctor himself would have been the
first to abandon his theory. That two such
upright men as Grewgious and Crisparkle
would have been parties to this wicked
deception, seems to me to be an utterly
untenable hypothesis, and that Grewgious

at least must have known of Edwin's escape,
if he did escape, is part and parcel of this
theory ; Crisparkle, with whom he was working to clear Neville, could not have been left
out of his confidence, and to have left Rosa in
ignorance would have been such an act of
cruelty as neither of these men could ever have
committed. That Drood's life was attempted
seems plain from the fact that his watch and
chain and scarf pin were discovered in the
weir by Crisparkle ; either, therefore, he was
really killed, or he managed to escape. If he
escaped, he and others who were aware of the
fact were almost as great criminals as Jasper,
inasmuch as they were wrecking Neville's
life ; legally, I think, they would also have
incurred a grave responsibility, as, knowing
that a murder had been attempted, they took
no steps to bring the wrong-doer to justice.
In face of these considerations, as there is no
necessity for proving that Edwin must have
survived, we are surely justified in concluding
that he was killed, as Dickens said.

There are, however, one or two difficulties
in the way of the unqualified acceptance of
the view that Drood was dead, and, as the

Americans say, stayed dead. There is first, the wrapper of the monthly parts, with its picture of Drood, as it is supposed, being discovered by Jasper in Mrs Sapsea's tomb. The man with the lantern *may* be Jasper, but it might also be Crisparkle (the costume is somewhat clerical in appearance); the other figure *may* be Edwin, or someone posing as Edwin, but, on the other hand, it might be Datchery, as Mr Walters suggests, or Neville in his own proper person. Considering the scanty materials which Collins had given to him by Dickens, when he was designing the wrapper, it would seem almost hopeless to attempt to deduce any valid argument from it, if it stood alone, but I think it must be considered in conjunction with other facts to which I shall draw attention. I had at one time a subordinate theory, to which I attached no importance, because I could not see the trend of it; it was, that the scene depicted might not represent Mrs Sapsea's tomb at all, and that the figures were not those of Jasper and a person masquerading as Edwin, as has been almost universally assumed, but Crisparkle discovering someone (I did not know

whom) in the medicinal herb-closet described
in Chapter x. Let me remark again that I
attached no importance to this guess at the
time, more particularly as I failed to understand its bearing on the story, but it had one
circumstance, although a very insignificant
one, to support it. That circumstance was,
that I could find no reason for the introduction by Dickens of the medicine closet into
the story, unless something were to be made
of it. It may be that the long passage in
Chapter x was merely descriptive, and nothing
else ; I do not think so, because Dickens
generally meant something by every detail
which he introduced. I observe, also, that
in his notes for this Chapter there is this
entry : " Minor Canon Corner. The Closet ? ",
a significant note when we remember that
Dickens was tabulating his materials and
scenes, and was hardly likely to jot down
purely descriptive matter leading to nothing.
It is also noteworthy that the closet in question
was a medicinal herb-closet, situated on an
upper staircase landing ; a " low and narrow
white-washed cell." Lastly, and this, I think,
might be significant, Dickens first describes

the dining-room closet, where the China Shepherdess kept her preserves, and reserves the description of the herb-closet for second place. The "note" speaks of one closet only, and the fact that two are described in the book, led me to believe that Dickens had some information to impart to his readers to which he desired to avoid drawing particular attention; the argument is the same as that which I have already used with reference to Jasper's diary, for what it may be worth in this connexion.

The theory which now, however, commends itself to me in regard to the herb-closet, enables me to offer a suggestion not only with reference to the enigmatical picture on the lower part of the cover, but also in connexion with the title of Chapter xiv, "When shall these three meet again?" It was contended by Proctor that Dickens evidently intended to convey to his readers, by means of this title, the suggestion that Jasper, Drood, and Neville *did* meet again. Mr Charles, on the other hand, points out a parallel between Jasper's crime and the murder committed by Macbeth, and he thinks that Dickens had Shakespeare's tragedy in his mind when he chose the title of Chapter XIV. He infers, therefore, that the quotation decisively proves that Edwin was murdered by Jasper, as Duncan was undoubtedly murdered by Macbeth, and he considers that the meaning that Proctor read into the quotation was unwarranted. In my view, both Proctor and Mr Charles are partly right, but they are also partly wrong. The chapter-heading chosen by Dickens is not a strictly accurate quotation ; what Shakespeare wrote was, " When shall *we* three meet again," and the line is to be found right at the commencement of *Macbeth*. It was spoken by one of the witches, all three of whom *do* meet again, on one other occasion at least. I think, therefore, that Dickens meant us to understand that Edwin, Neville, and Jasper were to meet again, and accordingly, that to this extent, Proctor was right. But I also think that Drood was murdered, so that, in the ordinary sense of the word, the three were not to meet again, so that, to this extent again, Mr Charles was right. When the three did meet, Edwin was dead, and lay hidden in

Mrs Sapsea's monument, whither Jasper had gone to recover the ring in order to obtain his final piece of evidence wherewith to incriminate Neville. But the latter, acting upon " information received," had been before him, and had secreted himself in the monument with the object of surprising Jasper, which he no doubt did very effectively. It is agreed on all hands that Neville was to die, and that he was to be murdered by Jasper, although there is no such agreement as to the manner or place of his death. I think the situation would be in the highest degree dramatic if the murder of Neville took place in Mrs Sapsea's monument, and I put forward the suggestion, therefore, that the picture on the cover was intended to represent Jasper entering the monument and discovering Neville. When we remember that at the end of Chapter xvi Crisparkle had suggested to the Dean that he would like to state that Neville would appear at Cloisterham whenever any new circumstance might come to light, and that the Dean had negatived the suggestion, and had shown himself generally opposed to Crisparkle affording Neville sanctuary, we can

understand that when it became necessary for
Neville to return to Cloisterham, it was advisable for the utmost secrecy to be observed,
not only because of the Dean's objections,
but also by reason of the very purpose of
Neville's return. What more natural, therefore, than that Crisparkle should have shel-
tered Neville secretly, and where could he have
hidden him so easily as in the medicine closet ?
There he would have been most effectively
hidden, and yet he would have been at hand
at a moment's notice to carry out the part he
was designed to play. To my mind, there is
nothing strained about this interpretation
either of the picture or of the title of Chapter
XIV, and as it enables us to connect the two
in a simple manner, as well as to find a use
for the medicine closet which Dickens described so carefully, and even elaborately, I
venture to assert that the theory I have pro-
posed at least requires careful consideration
before it is rejected.

One other point. In describing Jasper's
visit to Durdles, preparatory to the "nocturnal expedition," Dickens referred to "Two
skeleton journey-men...about to slash away

at cutting out the grave-stones of the next two people destined to die in Cloisterham. Likely enough, the two think little of that now, being alive, and perhaps merry. Curious, to make a guess at the two ;—or say at one of the two." That two people were to die is obvious, and that one was Edwin is almost equally obvious ; but whether the second was Neville, or whether he was Jasper himself, is not so easy to decide. To judge by the remark that perhaps they were merry, one would be inclined to conclude that Jasper could not have been the second, as the adjective which Dickens used is quite inapplicable to him. If, therefore, the second doomed man were Neville, we have further confirmation of my explanation of the picture, and the theory I have advanced in connexion with it.

Another objection to the theory that Drood is dead, and one which, before I knew of the existence of Dickens's notes, influenced me very considerably in favour of his escape, may be drawn from the conversation between Datchery and the opium woman. Datchery, if he was Edwin, knew of Jasper's opium habit ; but if he was any

one else, what ground have we for supposing
that he knew anything of it ? And yet,
I argued, he must have had some knowledge of it, for when the opium woman tells
Datchery : " I'll be honest with you beforehand, as well as after. It's opium " we
learn that " Mr Datchery, with a sudden
change of countenance, gives her a sudden
look." Now Edwin, on the occasion of his
meeting with this woman, had not only
recognised the opium look, but had actually
been told by her that she smoked opium.
Datchery's change of countenance when he
hears the word " opium," shows that he
had *some* knowledge either of the prior
meeting, or of Jasper's opium habit, and
I do not see that any other interpretation
can be put upon it ; we are therefore
enabled to draw a most important inference.
If Datchery is not Edwin, he can only have
heard of *this meeting* from one of two persons, the woman herself or Edwin ; about
that there can be no question. The argument is, that he has not met the woman
before, therefore he must have heard of the
meeting from Edwin ; ergo, Edwin, if not

still alive, and not Datchery, at least did not die on Christmas Eve. The alternative view, however, that Datchery knew nothing of the meeting, but did know otherwise of Jasper's opium habit, so that the mention by the woman of the word "opium" and her journey to Cloisterham to find out Jasper, cause him suddenly to change his countenance, is, in my opinion, the preferable one. It implies a somewhat close connexion between Datchery and Grewgious, which, in the circumstances, does not seem unlikely, although we have no definite knowledge of it, but it also involves, I think, an inconsistency which requires to be explained away. Such a close connexion as premised does not, of course, present any difficulty, and may, in fact, be assumed, if Datchery is either Helena, or Bazzard, or Grewgious's lawyer-friend, but as Jasper's opium habit was apparently known only to Edwin and Princess Puffer, it can, if Edwin be dead, presumably only have become known to Datchery by Jasper having been traced by someone to the opium den. Datchery would have seemingly thus learnt of the address of this den at the same time, so that his instructions to Deputy to find out where the opium woman lived would appear to be needless and therefore quite inexplicable. I am inclined to think that Grewgious had got to learn of Jasper's opium habit by some means which did not involve the tracing of the latter to the opium den, and (although this is pure guess-work) I suggest that we may have here an explanation of Grewgious's hint in Chapter XXI: "It is a business principle of mine, in such a case, not to close up any direction, but to keep an eye on every direction that may present itself. I could relate an anecdote in point, but that it would be premature." Whether this interpretation of Grewgious's anecdote be correct or not, I still believe that, by some means or other, he knew of Jasper's opium habit, and had informed Datchery of it, without, however, telling the latter of the opium woman's address, which he himself may or may not have known; this would account both for Datchery's obvious agitation, and for his instructions to Deputy, and I consider therefore that we are not obliged to assume that any information as to Jasper's opium habit had necessarily to be obtained from Edwin.

Proctor, whose theory compelled him to prove that Edwin was alive, made his best points, in my opinion, from the text itself. He called attention to very many passages where Dickens referred to Edwin after his disappearance, and pointed out that every one of them was consistent with the theory that Edwin was not dead. He also showed very cleverly that neither Rosa nor Grewgious ever definitely referred to Edwin as dead, and that all their numerous remarks concerning him were so worded as to leave their knowledge or belief upon the subject a perfectly open question. Upon this point I refer the reader to the articles by " Thomas Foster " in *Knowledge* for 1884, and content myself with observing that the able manner in which Proctor there deals with the evidence I am now considering would, in my view, carry conviction with it if we possessed only the materials which were then available to him. Since that time, however, Dickens's notes have been discovered, and other extraneous facts have been brought to light, all of which sufficiently explain the reasons for the ambiguous statements which Dickens put into the mouths of his characters, and personally I am convinced that his object in leaving Edwin's fate in doubt was to draw attention off his main " mystery " and to centre it around his subordinate one. It seems pretty obvious to me that had he allowed it to become known definitely that Edwin was dead, the interest in the book would at once have become focussed upon the manner of the detection of Jasper, which was exactly what Dickens would, in the circumstances, naturally have desired to avoid ; I have already drawn attention to this point, although from a somewhat different aspect, when considering the various titles which Dickens noted. I conclude, therefore, that all the evidence which Proctor laboriously brought together was purposely introduced by Dickens with a view to that very end, and that the imagination of the novelist successfully anticipated and forestalled the methods of the mathematician.

CHAPTER IV

PRINCESS PUFFER, AND OTHERS

HAD we a little more knowledge of the opium woman, I believe we should be able to obtain a glimpse of the complete plot, instead of the leading idea only, as I venture to think we now have. Unfortunately, she only enters upon the scene on three occasions, and in none of them is her undoubtedly important connexion with the story made apparent; let us see, however, whether we can catch any hint of her real *rôle* from the materials which we have.

By way of digression, let me remark that we know that Parts I and II were originally designed to contain four chapters each, and that, according to the notes, Chapter VIII, entitled "Mr Durdles and friend," was to contain a reference to the opium woman. Circumstances obliged Dickens, however, to transpose this chapter, which became Chapter V, the last in Part I, and he remodelled the second Part, which, as re-cast, contained Chapters VI to IX, the last, entitled " Birds in the Bush," being apparently new matter, as we find no reference to it in the notes proper. There is, however, on the back of the notes for Part II (I am assuming that Sir W. R. Nicoll's reproduction of them is exact in every detail) the following note : " Rosa's guardian ? *Done in No. II* " ; I take it, therefore, that by interpolating this chapter, Dickens got back to his scheme as originally planned, as until we reach Chapter XXI, entitled " A recognition," the Chapter numbers and titles in the notes agree with those of the book. Dickens must therefore have had the whole scheme well arranged in his mind, as, except for the transposition of what was originally Chapter VIII, and the interpolation of Chapters IX and XXI, the plan of the book agrees with that outlined in the notes.

The notes for Chapter VIII contained this sentence : " Carry through the woman of the first chapter," meaning, I take it, bring her upon the scene again here. No doubt,

Dickens realised that in its new position, this chapter could not appropriately contain any reference to the opium woman, and accordingly, although the remaining notes are fully utilised, Princess Puffer is entirely ignored. It is not until we reach Chapter XIV (" When shall these three meet again ? ") that she again makes her appearance, although the notes for that chapter do not mention her; from this I deduce that she has been " brought forward " from Chapter VIII, and that Dickens did not overlook her, or intend to bring her in either more or less often than three times in that portion of the book which we have.

Even when we first make her acquaintance in Chapter I, she either hates or suspects Jasper, because, although apparently oblivious to everything which is occurring (" she hands him the nearly empty pipe, and sinks back, turning over on her face"), we find her very wide awake indeed, for when Jasper drags forth the Lascar and the latter draws a phantom knife, she starts up and restrains and expostulates with him. In Chapter XXIII, she soliloquises thus : " I heard ye say once,

when I was lying where you're lying, and you
were making your speculations upon me,
' Unintelligible.' I heard ye say so, of two
more than me. But don't ye be too sure
always; don't ye be too sure, beauty ! "
Of her Jasper muses on this first occasion:
" What visions can *she* have ? Visions of
many butchers' shops, and public houses,
and much credit ? Of an increase of hideous
customers, and this horrible bedstead set
upright again, and this horrible court swept
clean ? What can she rise to, under any
quantity of opium, higher than that ? Eh ? "
I think it reasonably possible that Dickens
intended her to rise to something higher than
that subsequently, although from her un-
grammatical speech (" them two come in
after ye," " more nor three shillings," " I ses
to my poor self "), it is plain that she was a
woman of the lower classes. Note, by the
way, that she got " Heaven's hard drunk
for sixteen year afore " she took to opium
smoking; note also that Jasper was six and
twenty at the time of this scene, so that it
seems impossible that there can have been
any direct or personal connexion between the

two, other than opium smoking, prior to the beginning of the story.

We next meet with Princess Puffer on the occasion of her interview with Edwin on Christmas Eve. "Where do you come from?" he asks. "Come from London, deary," she replies. "Where are you going to?" he continues, and she answers "Back to London, deary. I came here, looking for a needle in a haystack, and I ain't found it." (The "needle in the haystack" was, of course, Jasper. "I'll not miss you twice," says she in Chapter XXIII.) She had evidently tried to follow him on the *previous* day, as we learn that on that morning Jasper was "early among the shopkeepers." She had no doubt passed the previous night, as she also stayed that night, at the Travellers Lodging House, and that was when and how Deputy became acquainted with her name and calling, because, as we learn in Chapter XXIII, she had only been once before in Cloisterham. As she came to find Jasper, and not to warn Edwin, as has been suggested, we cannot do otherwise than suppose that she had a sufficient motive for her long and

difficult journey. She had followed Jasper
and missed him ; he had therefore visited
her den a day or two previously, and had
the reason for her desire to trace him been
that she wished to give him some information, it is hardly likely that she would not
have given it to him when he was in London.
On this ground, therefore, and also because
of her behaviour on the occasion of her next
visit, we are justified in concluding that her
object in going to Cloisterham was a personal one ; she evidently wished to find out
who he was, where he lived, and what his
occupation was, but we are left entirely in
the dark as to her real motive. Plainly her
purpose was no friendly one, as we may
judge from her gesture when she subsequently sees him in the Cathedral, nor, for
the same reason, was it mere curiosity, nor
even cupidity. Hatred and desire for revenge
are the only grounds which satisfy all the
conditions, but even if we are entitled to
conclude that she nourished a secret hatred
against Jasper, we are no further advanced
unless we can assign some plausible reason
for it. In the book there is absolutely

nothing in the shape of a clue to this mystery, with one exception : the death shriek which Durdles had heard on the preceding Christmas Eve, the mention of which on the occasion of the nocturnal excursion, causes Jasper to ask " What do you mean ? " by way of a " very abrupt, and, one might say, fierce retort." That the shriek which Durdles heard was real I have not the slightest doubt, because otherwise I can imagine no reason for Dickens referring to it ; that it concerned Jasper, I also think is absolutely certain, for on no other ground is it possible to account for his sudden fierceness. The stretch of imagination necessary to enable us to connect together Jasper, the midnight death shriek, and the opium woman with her strong hatred of him, is not a very great one, and although I will not venture to advance any definite hypothesis, I nevertheless hazard a guess that she suspected him strongly of a crime already committed in which some relative or connexion of hers had figured as the victim.

I regard it as a curious fact, that whereas in the notes for Chapter VIII (which afterwards

became Chapter v), Dickens refers to Deputy
by name, noting "Deputy engaged to stone
Durdles nightly," in the notes for Chapter x (originally ix) we find this entry:
"remember there is a child"; there is no
other note preceded by the word "remember."
We find nothing at all about any child in
Chapter x, in fact, there is no mention of
any child at all anywhere in the book other
than Deputy, and we first meet with him
again at the end of Chapter xii, in the notes
for which Dickens records "keep the boy
suspended." Had the reference to the child
in the notes for Chapter x any special object?
Was Deputy to be the "child" in question,
and whose child was he? Was he related
to the opium woman, to Jasper, to the
person murdered on the preceding Christmas
Eve? It would be quite in keeping with
Dickens's methods if any, or even all, of these
surmises should turn out to be correct, and
it would at least be dramatic if Deputy, one
of the persons whose evidence was to be
used to convict Jasper, should happen to
be his own son by some woman he had
murdered. Obviously, if Deputy is engaged

to stone Durdles if he "catches him out after ten," it is because Dickens wants him to be out after that hour, so that it shall not appear unnatural for him to have observed Jasper on the night of the latter's expedition, but I very much doubt whether Dickens would have brought the boy on the scene without connecting him closely with some of the principal personages. I am disposed, therefore, to consider that Deputy was intended to play some other part in the *dénouement*, such as I have indicated above, but I can give no reason for the faith that is in me other than a subjective impression.

Now let us consider whether we can discover the object for Bazzard being introduced upon the scene. We have noted that he is a surly fellow, of uncouth appearance, and possessed of none of the qualifications which Datchery had, and I shall call attention to one or two curious points in connexion with him later on, but my present purpose is to discover his *rôle* in the drama which Dickens had imagined. We find in Chapter XI that Grewgious blames Edwin for not having acknowledged receipt of his copy of the will, and it seems to us quite natural that when Grewgious subsequently gives him the ring, he wakes Bazzard in order to make him a witness of the transaction. On the face of it, as I say, that seems quite natural in Grewgious, first and foremost a man of business and order : but if we look a little deeper, is it not possible to discern a hidden object in this little manoeuvre of Dickens, suggested, in fact, by his very attempt to make Grewgious's action seem natural ? We know that the only persons having knowledge of the nature of Grewgious's trust were himself, Edwin, and Bazzard ; Edwin, *ex hypothesi*, was dead, and Grewgious had not breathed a word to anyone of the ring, but yet we are told by Forster, that, so far as he knew, by means of this ring, the person murdered was to be identified, as well as the locality of the crime and the man who committed it. I accept some of this statement, but not all, as representing the fact, and my reason for discarding part of it is that it leaves no room for Durdles. For the moment, however, I am only concerned with Bazzard, and the part he played in the story, and I suggest that what

Dickens had in his mind was that Bazzard, of whom probably Jasper had made a tool, was to be the instrument leading to his destruction. Thus, Bazzard, having witnessed the handing of the ring to Edwin, knew that it had been in his possession the day before his death, a fact of which Jasper was unaware ; Bazzard, probably set to watch Jasper in London ("some hanger on of Staple" suggests Grewgious) turns traitor, and plays into Jasper's hands ; Jasper thus gets to hear of the existence of the ring and of the fact that it had been confided to Edwin. This provides him with the one piece of evidence against Neville for which he had been looking, and he accordingly resolves to recover the ring, with the object of placing it in Neville's possession. Meanwhile, Durdles, whose acquaintance had been cultivated by Datchery, had no doubt informed the latter of his nocturnal expedition with Jasper, or, it may be, Datchery had learned of this from Deputy. Datchery, with Grewgious's suspicions in his mind, had inferred that Jasper, who was "a wild beast and a brigand," had very obviously had some

object in exploring the Cathedral, and no
doubt when he learned from Durdles the full
truth of that expedition, his suspicions were
strengthened. He therefore set Durdles to
work searching by his accustomed methods,
and I suggest that the latter soon succeeded
in discovering Edwin's body, whether in
Mrs Sapsea's tomb or elsewhere hardly matters. My own view is that the ring was not
required to identify Edwin, because, contrary
to what everyone has assumed, I believe that
quicklime, *without the addition of water,* is not
a corrosive, but a preservative, and I think
that Dickens, who lived so near the Medway
Cement Works, must have known this, and
meant to make use of it. Is that, perhaps,
why he suggests that Edwin was disfigured ?
However that may be, and whether Dickens,
or his critics, or I, have been mistaken upon
this point, hardly matters for the moment ;
the important thing, to my mind, is, that
Edwin's body is discovered by Durdles, at
the instigation of Datchery, and removed ;
that Jasper, intending to recover the ring in
order to incriminate Neville, repairs to the
scene of his victim's burial, and is there

confronted by someone who has been waiting for him. Finding himself discovered, he turns and flees, rushing up the Cathedral tower, whither he is pursued by Crisparkle, the muscular Minor Canon so addicted to boxing, and Tartar, whose climbing propensities are specially brought to our notice by Dickens. Probably it was Neville who was hidden in Mrs Sapsea's tomb, and was murdered by Jasper before the latter was mastered by Crisparkle and Tartar, but that the purpose of the ring and the method of Jasper's discovery were intended to be worked out in the manner I have outlined, seems to me to be beyond doubt, as otherwise I feel that the words in Chapter XIII so often quoted with reference to the ring, can only be regarded as grossly exaggerated. " Among the mighty store of wonderful chains that are for ever forging, day and night, in the vast iron-works of time and circumstance, there was one chain forged in the moment of that small conclusion, riveted to the foundations of heaven and earth, and gifted with invincible force to hold and drag." If we merely assume that Jasper got to learn of the existence of the ring, and intended to remove it for the purpose of avoiding identification of the body, if and when discovered, could we not say of such a chain, in his own words " what a poor, mean, miserable thing it is ? " But if we adopt my suggestion, note how the chain lengthens out, and how much more worthy it becomes of Dickens's impressive description : the existence of the ring made known to Bazzard ; Bazzard employed by Grewgious to shadow Jasper, but turning traitor to his employer ; Jasper getting to hear from Bazzard of the ring, and of its having been entrusted to Edwin the day before his death ; his design to incriminate Neville ; his resolution to recover the ring for this purpose ; and, lastly, his stealthy visit to the place where Edwin lay buried, known, as he believes, only to himself, whereby his suspected guilt is finally proven, *by his own act*. A long chain, and a wonderful chain, which holds and drags with invincible force ; a chain which enables the prophecy recorded in his diary to be carried out to the letter ; a chain which, in fact, proves to me that the " curious, strong,

but incommunicable idea " which Dickens
had in his mind, when he wrote to Forster,
has finally been laid bare after forty-five
years of baffling pursuit. Truly the great
artist builded better than he knew !

While I am reasonably certain that the
chain which I have endeavoured to re-
construct must have comprised at least the
links which I have set out above, I am
persuaded that it must also have included
many others. To know all the intermediate
links would be to know Dickens's plot in all
its details, and I should be the first to admit
that this is a result which I have not achieved,
nor do I imagine that in the state of our
knowledge it will ever be definitely reached.
When one comes to examine critically the
several links which I have suggested as forming
the chain upon which Dickens laid such
emphasis, it becomes plain that they do
not connect up, while a careful consideration
of the text reveals so many facts which
might have been designed by Dickens to
be utilised as intermediate links, that the
difficulty experienced arises out of the super-
fluity, rather than the paucity, of material.

To take the latter point first, why did Sapsea take it upon himself in Chapter XII to answer for Jasper's neck ? Why were Miss Twinkleton and the Billickin not on speaking terms ? Why was Tartar a sailor, why was it necessary for him to resign his commission in the navy as a condition of succeeding to his uncle's estate, where was that estate, and why did Tartar have a yacht at Greenhithe ? It would be possible to go on multiplying enquiries of this sort almost indefinitely, and no doubt it would be an interesting exercise to extract the numerous hints which Dickens has given, and to consider their possible bearing upon the course of the story, but that is a task which would hardly be in place here, and I do not propose to pursue the subject any further.

On the other hand, however, it may perhaps serve some useful purpose to indicate some of the more obvious gaps in the chain, and although I can hardly hope to be successful in supplying them satisfactorily, yet other enquirers may possibly be able to profit indirectly by my guesses. If my theory be correct, we know the two ends of the chain with a reasonable degree of certainty. At the one end we find the ring given to Edwin by Grewgious in the presence of Bazzard, a totally unnecessary witness, and Edwin's determination to let the jewels " lie unspoken of in his breast," so that they were buried with him in whatever hiding-place Jasper deposited his corpse ; at the other, we see Jasper secretly visiting that hiding-place, upon information procured from Bazzard regarding the possession of the ring by Edwin, and thus providing evidence, otherwise unobtainable, of his knowledge of the crime. But between these two ends there is a considerable hiatus, which it is extremely hard to fill, not only by reason of the known facts, but also on account of the difficulty in imagining how Grewgious and his associates were to know exactly when Jasper had got to hear of the ring, so as to be able to utilise their knowledge for bringing about his ultimate discomfiture in the manner suggested. By "known facts " I mean Jasper's connexion with the opium woman, her hatred of him, Deputy's aston- ishment when he observes her threatening gestures, Bazzard's "Thorn of Anxiety," and so on; each and all of these facts must have been intended by Dickens to have some definite bearing upon the development of the story, and I cannot but think that they were to form links in the wonderful chain which was eventually to bring Jasper to justice. However that may be, it seems absolutely necessary, if we are to know anything more than the barest outline of the plot, to suggest some explanation at least of the means by which Jasper and Neville were to be brought together in Mrs Sapsea's monument, to Jasper's undoing, and I therefore put forward, with the greatest diffidence, the following tentative explanation.

It is obvious that Durdles, with his unaccountable gift, was designed to discover Edwin's body; the ring, although it might have served as a means of identification, could hardly have been a means of discovery, as we know that it was contained in a case, so that it would have failed to attract attention by the sparkling of its stones. Durdles's search was no doubt a systematic one, undertaken at the instigation of Datchery, and it appears likely that Deputy intervened in some way, as in Chapter v we are significantly told that he was " skirmishing nearer, as suspecting that Treasure was about to be discovered, which may somehow lead to his own enrichment, and the delicious treat of the discoverers being *hanged by the neck, on his evidence,* until they are dead." That Mrs Sapsea's monument was the hiding-place, is clearly deducible from the information given, in the same chapter, by Durdles to Jasper, that there was a free space of six feet inside its wall.

To this monument Durdles had access, because we are told in Chapter iv, after Sapsea had handed him the key, " Durdles keeps the keys of his works mostly " ; there is no difficulty, therefore, in explaining how Durdles's discovery was verified, or how Neville was introduced into the monument on a subsequent occasion. Jasper, on the other hand, obtained admission to the monument, on the night of his discovery, in the same manner, whatever that may have been, as on the night of the murder.

Jasper, I have assumed, got to learn of

the ring from or through Bazzard, but whether
by accident, or through Bazzard's treachery,
or in execution of Grewgious's design, it
is impossible to say. The probabilities seem
to me to point in the direction of a treacherous
disclosure, or at least an accidental one,
Dickens's idea being based, as I think, on
the notion of a man's crime finding him
out. Consequently, if Fate could be made
to furnish the final link which man's efforts
were incapable of forging, we are probably
justified in assuming that Dickens would
have preferred that solution. Let us suppose,
then, that Jasper learned from Bazzard,
in some manner, that the ring was in Edwin's
pocket at the time of his murder, and let
us also suppose that Bazzard had disclosed
to Jasper where Rosa was hiding, which
information he would have obtained quite
naturally as the Billickin's relative. Jasper's
first impulse would certainly have been to
call upon Rosa at once, with the object of
further pressing his suit, under threat of
accomplishing Neville's destruction if she
still refused him. If Helena were at the
Billickin's at the time of Jasper's visit, which

seems not unlikely, she, who would not have been afraid of him " under any circumstances," would have encouraged Rosa to defy him, and if thereupon he had boasted that he had at last obtained the one wanting link necessary for the establishment of Neville's guilt, Helena would no doubt have hurried off to Grewgious and informed him of the danger. The latter must have either already known, or immediately surmised, that Jasper had at last obtained knowledge of the existence of the ring, and it would at once have occurred to him that Jasper would surely take the earliest opportunity of getting possession of it in order to incriminate Neville conclusively. Thereupon, no doubt, Grewgious, Neville, and Tartar must have hurried off to Cloisterham, Neville being temporarily secreted in Crisparkle's medicine closet, and subsequently introduced, with the assistance of Durdles, into the Sapsea monument, when night fell. Grewgious, Tartar, and Crisparkle would probably have remained within call, and have watched Jasper's movements, undoubtedly expecting him to be surprised into flight as soon as he discovered that Neville knew his secret, but it seems to me that such an expectation took no account of Jasper's villainous character, which would have caused him to attempt to murder Neville rather than allow his guilt to be exposed. This design, I imagine, he was to have carried into execution with dramatic effect, and it would probably only have been after leaving the Sapsea monument that he would have become aware that there were others on his track. Thereupon, no doubt, he would have attempted to escape by flight, and, being hunted into the Cathedral, would finally have been captured by Tartar and Crisparkle, after a desperate struggle, and lodged in gaol, where, in accordance with Dickens's expressed intentions, he would have written the full story of his temptations and crimes, and have paid the final penalty.

CHAPTER V

MINOR MATTERS

Now that I have traced out Dickens's central theme, and sketched in the main lines upon which it was to have been developed, and have also, as I think, definitely identified Datchery, it remains to discuss several of the many subordinate questions which present themselves to anyone reading *Edwin Drood*. In doing this, I do not propose to attempt to follow any logical sequence; indeed, by reason of the variety of subjects requiring explanation, I do not think this is possible, and I will therefore examine such points only as appear of importance, and in the sequence in which they present themselves to my mind.

In the first place, what bearing, if any, have Dickens's proof-revisions upon my main thesis, and what object had he in view in making them? We know that three monthly Parts had been issued during Dickens's life,

that three others had been written, and that
he had himself corrected the proofs up to
and including Chapter XXI.   We also know
that he had expressed some misgiving to
his sister-in-law respecting the " Datchery
assumption " in the fifth number (Chapter XVIII), and it is not an unreasonable
inference to draw, that the revisions which
he made in that number, as also probably
those in the succeeding number, were directed
to the removal of the causes for this misgiving, so far as that might be done at that
stage.   Some of the revisions, of course,
were doubtless made from a purely literary
point of view, and therefore have no bearing
upon the matter in hand, but others were
quite evidently made from a different motive,
and it is these to which I intend to direct
attention.

The first of these, I think, occurs in
Chapter XVII, and consists in the deletion
of a few sentences, commencing with the
words " Mr Crisparkle rose " and ending
" to be undertaken by a layman."   It seems
to me that Dickens wished to hide, for the
moment, the connexion which evidently

existed between Jasper and Honeythunder;
the latter was, as I have already surmised,
to be one of the trio or quartet which,
under the leadership or guidance of Jasper,
was to be actively engaged in fastening the
murder of Edwin upon Neville. That Honeythunder, the blustering philanthropist, was
clearly intended by Dickens to play such a
part, appears to me to follow almost naturally
from the characteristics with which Dickens
endowed him, and it is not surprising, therefore, that in order to divert attention from
him for a time, and possibly, also, with a
view to delaying the *dénouement*, he revised
his original intention of acquainting the reader
with the existence of this iniquitous collaboration. Exactly how Honeythunder was to
participate in the plot which Jasper was
weaving, I cannot surmise, but that such
a *rôle* was assigned to him, does not, I venture
to assert, admit of much doubt.

The next excision appears to me to have
no reference to the plot and therefore to call
for no remark, but the following one is in a
different case. The words deleted are these,
which occur in a conversation between Neville

and Crisparkle : Neville says " It seems a little hard to be so tied to a stake and innocent ; but I don't complain." " And you must expect no miracle to help you " said Mr Crisparkle compassionately. " No, sir, I know that." I think that Dickens felt that if Neville was to expect no *miracle* to help him, it was open to the reader to surmise that active steps to the same end were being taken by someone, and that consequently there might have been aroused a sub-conscious feeling that Datchery was working in conjunction with Grewgious to bring Jasper to book, in order to clear Neville. As it is my opinion that Datchery *was* so engaged, and that he was Grewgious's legal acquaintance, I can well understand that Dickens thought it advisable to delete the passage, and I can imagine no other ground for his decision.

I fail entirely to appreciate the motive which actuated Dickens in making his next excision. Neville had stated that on the advice of Crisparkle, he had taken up the difficult profession of the law, and Dickens had made it plain that Crisparkle had either given or lent him the necessary books. These he studied under the guidance and with the help of the latter, and Dickens informs his reader that " the Minor Canon's duties made these visits of his difficult to accomplish, and only to be compassed at intervals of many weeks. *But they were as serviceable as they were precious to Neville Landless.*" The words which Dickens struck out are those which I have italicised, and I am at a loss to suggest any reason for his doing so ; they seem to me to be absolutely harmless, and much less objectionable from the point of view of the disclosure of Crisparkle's strong interest in the exculpation of Neville than many other phrases which Dickens allowed to stand.

Much of the remainder of the conversation between Neville and Crisparkle on the same occasion was deleted by Dickens, and the sentences which he struck out have been relied upon as affording support to the Helena-Datchery theory, upon the ground that Dickens feared that the identification might thereby be made manifest. Naturally, having rejected this theory, I am

compelled to search for some other reason,
but I frankly admit that I have discovered
none which satisfies me entirely. Perhaps
Dickens considered that at that stage of his
story they were unduly eulogistic of Helena,
and that Crisparkle's admiration of and love
for her were growing too quickly to seem
entirely natural. At any rate, I do not
think that they were deleted on the ground
that they were likely to enable Helena to
be identified as Datchery, because Dickens
allowed several important sentences to stand,
which, to my mind, militate strongly against
the Helena-Datchery theory. Upon this
point, however, I refrain from dogmatising,
being content to allow the evidence which
I may have adduced in support of the lawyer-
Datchery theory to be weighed against that
thought to be afforded for the other view
by the words in question.

All the other excisions in this chapter
relate to Grewgious, and were made, I consider, with a view to hiding from the reader
that he was keeping a watch on Jasper;
they are set out in detail in Sir W. R. Nicoll's
book, to which I refer the reader.

In Chapter XVIII we come upon some alterations of considerable interest. I attach no great weight to the excision either of the waiter's remark to Datchery : " Indeed, I have no doubt that we could suit you that far, however particular you might be," or of Dickens's comment upon Datchery's search for the Cathedral ; but I consider that it is impossible to over-rate the importance of the words " with a second look of some interest " which Dickens deleted upon second thoughts, when describing how Datchery regarded Jasper's window, upon Deputy, somewhat unnecessarily, pointing it out to him. If it was Dickens's desire to avoid raising a suspicion that Datchery was at Cloisterham with the express object of observing Jasper and collecting evidence against him (and that is what I understand to be the real purport of the fear which he expressed to his sister-in-law), I can readily appreciate his object in removing this particular sentence when revising the proofs, and I am strengthened in this view by the other excisions which he made. For instance, he deleted the whole paragraph wherein he had made Datchery draw from

Mrs Tope the recital of the tragedy, and the whole of the long conversation between Datchery and Sapsea on the same subject, as well as the indirect references to the law; further, the reminder to Deputy that he owes him a job also disappears. I have not the slightest doubt that Dickens felt he had prematurely disclosed Datchery's interest in Drood's disappearance, and, on reflection, decided, for the time being, to conceal the real purpose of his mission; he therefore struck out not only all reference to Drood's murder, but also all conversation about Jasper, and, finally, the few words relating to Datchery's intention to visit Durdles. With all these excisions made from this chapter, as Dickens intended, Datchery's reflection at the end of it would have had much more point; as the book now stands, we find no difficulty in agreeing that he had had a rather busy afternoon, inasmuch as he had found lodgings in the very place he had been directed to seek for them, had made the acquaintance of Jasper, Sapsea, Deputy, and Durdles, had learned that Deputy heartily disliked Jasper, and that there were

grave suspicions entertained about somebody
with reference to the murder. Dickens's mis-
givings were indeed justified, and I think
the result would have been much more
artistic if Forster had not disregarded
Dickens's emendations.

In Chapter xx there is only one phrase
struck out, and that, I think, was done
because Dickens noticed that the purport of
the phrase was repeated a few lines lower.
In Chapter xxi several sentences were deleted,
which might conceivably have directed attention to what Dickens wished to keep secret,
namely, the collaboration of Grewgious and
Crisparkle in the steps which were being
taken to have Jasper kept under observation, and also probably the fact that any
observation at all was being kept; I can
see no other reason for these excisions upon
any view whatever.

I think it may fairly be concluded that
Dickens's proof-revisions, with one exception,
which is indifferent, all tend to strengthen
my main position, so that from yet another
point of view my theories receive confirmation.

The next matter which I propose to deal
with, is the part played by Grewgious, and
the explanation of his conduct on a memorable occasion. I call attention, in the first
place, to the conversation which he had with
Jasper, set out in full at the end of Chapter x ;
the whole of it is of more or less importance
but I lay special stress upon the concluding
words : Grewgious had said, " God bless
them both." " God save them both " cried
Jasper. " I said, bless them," remarked
Grewgious. " I said, save them " returned
the other. " Is there any difference ? "
This incident must have stuck in Grewgious's
memory, so that when the disappearance
occurred, the words used by Jasper no doubt
came back to him. Add to this, first, that
when he went to Cloisterham at Christmas,
he must have heard from Rosa about her
instinctive repulsion from Jasper, as well as
the incident of the dinner-party ; probably
also she told him how Jasper had spied
upon Edwin and her on the occasion of their
last meeting. Again, we are told that Grewgious, before calling on Jasper a day or two
after the murder, had just left Helena, and

we can readily believe that under his cross-examination, if, indeed, any were necessary, she had told him what Rosa might have omitted, namely, that Jasper was in love with her. A man less shrewd than Grewgious might have had his suspicions aroused, even if he had learned nothing more than this ; but he did know something more, he knew that Rosa and Edwin had agreed to part, and that no information had yet been given to Jasper about this fact ; that the mention of a betrothal by deceased parents had caused Jasper's lips to grow white ; that, so far as Jasper was aware, Rosa had hinted no wish to be released from Edwin ; and that Jasper thought that at Christmas pre-parations were to be completed for the wedding in May. Whether he knew any-thing further is a matter of surmise. The murder took place on December 24th ; Grewgious was to dine with Rosa on the 25th, and he only appears on the scene on the night of the 27th. He had ample time in which not only to interview Rosa and Helena, but also to make enquiries in other quarters, and it is quite conceivable that Deputy, who

was a night-bird, might have seen Jasper on
the night of the murder, and have somehow
been discovered and interviewed by Grewgious. I think, however, that it is quite
unnecessary to make any such assumption,
as the manner in which Grewgious opens his
attack on Jasper seems to me only to warrant
the view that he had gauged Jasper's villainous character, and that, having discovered
a possible motive, he had inferred the very
likely probability of Jasper's criminality.
As a barrister by training, he dealt with
his man in a non-committal way at first,
making his soundings and feeling his ground
as he went along ; not absolutely antago-
nistic at the start, but merely stern and
suspicious. (The title of Fildes's illustration
of the scene is " Mr Grewgious has his suspicions.") Then, finding that Jasper fences
with him (" Do you suspect him ? " asks
Grewgious. " I don't know what to think.
I cannot make up my mind," replies Jasper).
Grewgious determines upon a coup, the result
of which will afford him moral certainty of
Jasper's guilt or innocence. The coup comes
off, and Jasper, in Grewgious's eyes, stands

convicted, a self-confessed murderer ; hence-
forth he is a man to be avoided, feared, and
watched. The murder which Grewgious feels
assured has been committed, is to be verified
in the first place, and his next task will then
be to prove Jasper's guilt, and to demand
retribution. Grewgious, the upright man,
indefatigable in seeking out right and doing
right, has a plain duty before him from that
moment, and the whole of his subsequent
conduct is consistent with his moral conviction of Jasper's guilt, and with his
inability for the moment to establish it by
legal means. Hence his recourse to his legal
adviser, his employment of Bazzard as a
watch-dog, his enlistment of Crisparkle's aid,
his appeal to Tartar for help. If he had
known, he would have struck immediately ;
he did not know, he merely suspected, and
therefore he set to work to obtain evidence
from any and every likely quarter. That
he eventually obtained it, there can be no
doubt, but certainly not in the way he
anticipated ; it was the " miracle," which
Crisparkle had regarded as impossible, which
ultimately came to pass, and Jasper finally

furnished the one necessary damning piece
of evidence which all Grewgious's efforts had
been unavailing to discover.

Hitherto I have dealt with Bazzard somewhat summarily, but I think it necessary to
consider this character a little more at length
here, because I feel convinced that he, too,
had his mystery, although I am of opinion
that we have not enough evidence to enable
us to fathom it. He is first referred to in
Chapter IX, on the occasion of Grewgious's
call on Rosa. " I have no other engagement
at Christmas-time," he remarks, " than to
partake, on the twenty-fifth, of a boiled turkey
and celery sauce with a—with a particularly
angular clerk I have the good fortune to
possess, whose father, being a Norfolk farmer,
sends him up (the turkey up), as a present to
me, from the neighbourhood of Norwich."
The first point calling for remark in this
statement of Grewgious's, is, what was he going
to call Bazzard when he stopped himself ?
Secondly, why had he the " good fortune "
to possess such a clerk, who, as we afterwards see, was in reality a surly, ill-man-
nered person, and tolerably conceited ?

Thirdly, why was it necessary for the reader to be informed that Bazzard's father was a Norfolk farmer ?

We next meet with Bazzard in Chapter XI, when Edwin calls upon Grewgious. The latter remarks, " It's fortunate I have so good a fire ; but Mr Bazzard has taken care of me." " No, I haven't " said Mr Bazzard at the door. " Ah ! then it follows that I must have taken care of myself without observing it," replies Grewgious, taking no notice, it will be observed, of Bazzard's rude contradiction. Then follow the invitation of Bazzard to dinner, in accepting which he is equally uncouth, and Grewgious's instructions to him concerning the meal, about which he afterwards remarks to Edwin, " I was a little delicate, you see, about employing him in the foraging or commissariat department. Because he mightn't like it." " He seems to have his own way, sir," remarked Edwin. " His own way ? " returned Mr Grewgious, " O dear no ! Poor fellow, you quite mistake him. If he had his own way, he wouldn't be here." Later on in the same chapter, after being told that

Bazzard had done his work of consuming
meat and drink in a workmanlike manner,
though mostly in speechlessness, we find
that the first toast is drunk to his success,
and that the nearest Grewgious can get to
an intelligible sentiment is, may the thorn
of anxiety come out at last. Thereupon
Bazzard frowns at the fire, and goes through
various antics which Dickens describes, remarking, "I follow you, sir, and I thank
you." We then get Grewgious's whispered
apology, with the peculiar reason that if
Bazzard had not been placed first, he might
not have liked it, and after that we hear
nothing more of him until the end of the
chapter, where we learn that he awoke himself by his own snoring, and sat apoplectically
staring at vacancy. (Imagine such conduct
on the part of Datchery!) Bazzard then
witnesses the handing over of the ring to
Edwin, and immediately disappears, to return
no more in person upon the scene.

In Chapter xx, however, he forms the
subject of a long conversation between Grewgious and Rosa, with regard to which the
first point I have to notice is that Dickens

wrote the following explanation: "It was not hard to divine that Mr Grewgious had related the Bazzard history thus fully, at least quite as much for the recreation of his ward's mind from the subject that had driven her there, as for the gratification of his own tendency to be social and communicative." I think that it is a perfectly fair inference to draw from the explanation which Dickens thus volunteers, that the real reason for the Bazzard history being thus fully set out was *not* that stated by Dickens, but that, on the contrary, he had some information to impart to the reader which he wanted to bring in as naturally as possible, so as not to make it too conspicuous. I am confirmed in my opinion that this view is correct, first, by the fact that Dickens's original title for this Chapter was "Let's talk," an expression which he puts, wholly unnecessarily, into Grewgious's mouth at least three times in the course of this conversation; secondly, by Rosa's query, "How came you to be his Master?", a question about which Grewgious is made to observe "a question that *naturally* follows," whereas, in fact, there is nothing natural about it at all; and thirdly, because Rosa finally enquires, *à propos de bottes*, as I think, " Is the tragedy named ? " The conversation is too long to be set out here *in extenso*, but it is well worth reading with the greatest care, as in my view it not only deals with the Bazzard mystery, but may also have been intended to throw some light upon the ultimate development of the story, although I fail to evolve a satisfactory theory. It is interesting to note, however, that when Rosa suggests, without any apparent justification, that Bazzard must be very fond of Grewgious, the latter replies, " He bears up against it with commendable fortitude if he is," from which we must conclude that Grewgious does *not* think that he is ; why, therefore, does Grewgious retain him as his clerk, if clerk he be ? The explanation of how the employment originated appears to me to be somewhat weak, and I am inclined to hazard the guess that the Norfolk farmer, of whom we now hear for the second time, was to have been introduced to us in person at a later stage. The main point, however, around

which the conversation centres, is Bazzard's
play ; a tragedy, bearing the dreadfully
appropriate name of "The Thorn of Anxiety."
I cannot help thinking that this tragedy,
with its suggestive name, must have been
intended to play some important part in
the development, and I throw out the suggestion, for what it is worth, that in some
unexpected manner, it was to have formed
a link in the chain which held and dragged
Jasper to his doom. I should be the first
to admit that I am making a mere guess,
and that it is as likely as not that my surmise is utterly wrong, but at the same time
I cannot believe that Dickens would have
dealt with the subject at the length and in
the careful manner he did, if it were merely
superfluous matter entirely unconnected with
his main plot. I note, by the way, that the
tragedy was named, and therefore probably
completed, before Edwin's death, so that it
is hardly possible that it contained any
incidents calculated to impart any information to Jasper, even if it did eventually
"come out " and were seen by him. In
conclusion, I am of opinion that upon the

materials which we possess, the Bazzard
mystery is insoluble, and I very much doubt
whether a satisfactory solution will ever be
offered.

I hold a similar opinion with regard to
the " manner of the murder," the discovery
of which was to be prepared by Chapter XII;
I have read this chapter again and again,
and am hardly any wiser now than when
I first read it. There are certainly one or
two clues, but they are too shadowy and
indefinite to warrant any detailed theory
being advanced, except with the utmost
diffidence. The first difficulty we encounter
is the *locus in quo*; we are told in Chapter v
that Jasper came upon Durdles leaning
against the iron railing of the burial ground
enclosing it from the old cloister-arches,
from which, I think, we are fairly entitled
to deduce that Mrs Sapsea's monument was
situated outside the Cathedral precincts.
(Note, by the way, that Drood's father lay
beneath the sarcophagus immediately adjoin-
ing Mrs Sapsea.) When we come to the
nocturnal expedition, we learn that Jasper
and Durdles descended into the crypt by

a small side door, of which Durdles had the
key, and that they locked themselves in.
Reference to Chapter IV shows us that the
three keys which Durdles produced to Jasper
were all keys of monuments ; two of these
he put back into his capacious pockets, and
the third was tied up in his dinner-bundle.
Jasper and Durdles do not remain in the
crypt, to which they had descended by
rugged steps ; they are to ascend the great
tower, and on the steps by which they rise
to the Cathedral, Durdles pauses for new
store of breath. That these are the same
steps as they descended by, seems to me to
be certain, as Durdles " opens the door at the
top of the steps with the key he has already
used...and so emerges on the Cathedral
level." Then Jasper "fumbles among his
pockets for a key confided to him that will
open an iron gate, so as to enable them to
pass to the staircase of the great tower."
So far, five keys have been mentioned ;
three belonging to monuments (one of which
was Mrs Sapsea's), another belonging to the
crypt door, and the last opening the iron gate
giving entrance to the staircase of the tower.

Next we find Jasper taking possession of
Durdles's dinner-bundle, in which, as we saw
in Chapter IV, he had deposited the key of
Mrs Sapsea's monument. The pair then
ascend the tower, and Jasper contemplates
" especially that stillest part of " the scene
" which the Cathedral overshadows." The
iron gate is locked after their descent, after
which Durdles falls asleep at once, and
dreams. He dreams that something touches
him, and that something falls from his hand
(say, at a venture, the key of the crypt door) ;
then, something clinks and gropes about (say,
at another venture, Jasper searching for the
key of Mrs Sapsea's tomb, and identifying it
by its note) ; then Durdles slumbers undisturbed until two o'clock, when he wakes and
finds the key of the crypt door lying close by.
Seeing that it was mid-winter, that Jasper
had sat at his piano for two or three hours
after it had grown dark, and had then
repaired to Durdles's house, the expedition
could not have started later than eight
o'clock ; assuming that it lasted, so far as
Durdles was concerned, for an hour, we
deduce that Jasper had not less than five

hours of undisturbed freedom in which to
make his separate investigations and pre-
parations. He had in his own pocket the
key of the iron gate leading to the great
tower ; he had evidently taken from Durdles
the key of the crypt door, which the latter
subsequently found on the ground ; and it
is possible that he had abstracted the key of
Mrs Sapsea's monument either from Durdles's
dinner-bundle, or from his pocket. It is
probable, also, that Jasper had thoroughly
searched his bundle, because, prior to depart-
ing, Durdles said, " Let me get my bundle
right, Mister Jarsper, and I'm with you,"
and as he tied it afresh, he became conscious that he was very narrowly observed.
What did Jasper do with the three keys and
the five hours ? That he must have been
outside the Cathedral precincts is clear from
the rage into which he fell when he imagined
that Deputy had followed them when they first
came, or had been prowling near them ever
since, but that he had been engaged in cart-
ing lime from Durdles's yard to Mrs Sapsea's
monument seems to me to be such an incon-
ceivably risky procedure for a respectable

choirmaster to adopt, that I cannot admit
that Dickens ever imagined it. It is quite
possible that he visited Mrs Sapsea's monument in order to make his arrangements
there for the hiding of Edwin's body ; knowing, as he did, of Durdles's peculiar faculty for
unearthing buried objects, it is only reasonable
to think that Jasper would have chosen a
hiding place *outside* the crypt, and therefore
presumably beyond the reach of Durdles's
ordinary activities. But that he spent five
hours in the monument I consider quite
unlikely, more particularly as he possessed
the key of the iron gate leading to the tower,
and I suggest that some of his time at least
was passed on the summit of the tower.
We are told in Chapter xiv that on the
morning after the murder it was seen " that
the hands of the Cathedral clock are torn off ;
that lead from the roof has been stripped
away, rolled up, and blown into the close ;
and that some stones have been displaced
upon the summit of the great tower." Is it
drawing too much upon our imagination to
suppose that Jasper loosened the lead from
the roof, so that he might wrap up Edwin's

corpse in it, and thus throw it over into the close without shattering the body and leaving bloodstains behind, and that the stones were displaced by him in order to facilitate this method of disposing of the corpse ? We are told by Jasper himself in Chapter XXIII that there was "no struggle, no consciousness of peril, no entreaty," and we also know that Dickens intended Edwin to be strangled by Jasper either with his neck-tie or the long black silk scarf which he ultimately gave him. All the facts that we know, and are ever likely to know, appear to me to point to the "manner of the murder" having been somewhat as follows: Edwin and Jasper ascend the tower together after twelve o'clock on Christmas Eve to observe the effect of the storm, the former having probably previously drunk some wine that had been drugged ; Jasper puts his own scarf round Edwin's neck on the pretext of protecting him from the wind, and immediately strangles him with it, without Edwin being conscious of any peril, or making any struggle or entreaty. Jasper rolls his body up in the lead covering which he had previously loosened, with this object, from the roof of the tower, removes a few stones out of the way, and rolls the body over into the close below. In its descent it strikes against the face of the clock, catches on the hands, and by its weight drags them from their spindle, this being possibly what Jasper alluded to when he cried in his trance, " and yet I never saw *that* before." He next abstracts from the corpse of his victim the watch and chain and pin (all the jewellery of which he had knowledge), and deposits Edwin's remains in some safe hiding-place, in all probability, Mrs Sapsea's monument.

I am aware that some of this has been suggested before, and that, at the best, it is pure surmise, but I think that I have brought several facts into prominence which have hitherto escaped attention, and which materially strengthen this hypothetical explanation. I regard as metaphorical only the two statements of Jasper which do not square with this explanation, namely, " To think how often fellow-traveller, and yet not know it ! To think how many times he went the journey, and never saw the road," and this other, " It was a journey, a difficult and dangerous

journey....A hazardous and perilous journey,
over abysses where a slip would be destruction." I think that the fact that he refers
to " a journey " plainly indicates that he is
talking in metaphor, and accordingly I see no
real difficulty in accepting the explanation of
the manner of the murder advanced above, as
the correct one. I doubt whether we shall
ever have another offered which fits in better
with the known facts.

There is one fact which might be considered as strongly opposed to the correctness
of this theory, and that is, that towards the
end of Chapter XVI, Dickens himself, in considering the possibility of Neville's having
committed the murder, suggests that Drood
might have been so artfully disfigured, or
concealed, or both, that the murderer hoped
identification to be impossible. My answer
to this is, that if at the end of the same
chapter, Dickens makes Jasper produce his
diary, the entry in which discloses Dickens's
principal idea, it is not unlikely that he considered that the best way to conceal a secret
was, to use an Hibernianism, to expose it.
Sardou, it will be remembered, in one of his

comedies, makes the whole of his plot turn upon a missing document, which was quite safely hidden in a most conspicuous place[1]. I take it that Dickens anticipated Sardou, in that he fearlessly disclosed what he most desired to hide, and that his artifice was successful is proved by the controversies which have raged for many years around his book. I consider, therefore, that the objection to which I have alluded possesses no real weight.

It would be possible to write many pages respecting other characters and incidents; Durdles, for instance, and Deputy, and Tope, whose name was originally to have been Peptune (curiously like the word peptone which one finds in the chemistry books) and the Billickin, Bazzard's cousin divers times removed, with her empty third floor to let; Tartar, also, with his cool head and strong arm, and sailor-like climbing abilities, and Crisparkle, the athletic Minor Canon, with his swimming and boxing propensities. But however interesting these characters

[1] The idea probably originated with E. A. Poe, who used it most effectively in his story "The Purloined Letter."

might be to study, I doubt whether we should ever learn any more through them of the true nature of Dickens's plot, and as this was the object with which I set out when I started to write this little book, I do not propose to carry my investigations any further. It is for the reader to say whether I have succeeded in elucidating any of the difficult problems which Dickens's book presents, and if only one of the several suggestions which I have advanced should meet with general accept- ance, I shall esteem myself amply repaid for the labour which I have expended upon it.

For EU product safety concerns, contact us at Calle de José Abascal, 56–1°, 28003 Madrid, Spain or eugpsr@cambridge.org.

 www.ingramcontent.com/pod-product-compliance
Ingram Content Group UK Ltd.
Pitfield, Milton Keynes, MK11 3LW, UK
UKHW012328130625
459647UK00009B/126